THE KINDNESS OF COLOR

Janice is a friend of mine and she has written a book full to the brim with passion, truth and insight. The lessons you will learn as you turn these pages will help you not only understand the past, but will influence your future.

BOB GOFF
New York Times Bestselling Author of *Love Does*, *Everybody Always* and *Dream Big*

Beautifully written, an American story of the courage, patriotism and resilience of two Orange County families.

HONORABLE FREDERICK AGUIRRE
Judge, Superior Court of Orange County (retired)

The Kindness of Color is a beautifully crafted true and inspiring story of how the cross-cultural cooperation between two oppressed families and communities of color in Orange County, California, during the World War II era, led to a landmark case of public-school desegregation at the state and national levels. At a time when transformational courses in ethnic studies are being mandated at both of these levels, Janice Munemitsu's book is ideally suited to being a curricular staple.

DR. ART HANSEN
Emeritus Professor of History and Asian American Studies,
California State University, Fullerton

The Kindness of Color offers an engaging and unique true account of 1940s history. The book follows two immigrant families—one Japanese American and one Mexican American—as they confront racism in California during and after World War II. Munemitsu relies on family stories, personal interviews, and extensive research to document her narrative, but she doesn't stop there. She shows how kindness and respect provide an antidote to bigotry and how one act of kindness can lead to another, until the whole world is changed.

WINIFRED CONKLING
Author, *Sylvia & Aki*

In *The Kindness of Color*, Janice Munemitsu provides the true story of two families behind the *Mendez v. Westminster* case that led to the desegregation of California public schools in 1947. By divine intervention, the Mendez and Munemitsu families met while confronting many forms of racism during World War II. Through it all, the unconditional kindness they received from others and returned to others ultimately proved to be a force for healing and change.

The Kindness of Color is a compelling work that shows how individual acts of kindness by many in the midst of gross injustice provided healing and encouragement, not just to these two families, but also brought meaningful change to the community, state, and eventually the nation. As the former superintendent of the Santa Ana Unified School District during the naming and construction of the first school named after the Mendez family, Gonzalo & Felicitas Mendez Fundamental Intermediate School in 1997, I believe this book should serve as a primer of imperative justice and be required reading in civics and history classes across America.

AL MIJARES, PHD
Orange County Superintendent of Schools

Kindness is being given a box of vegetables and fruit from a friend's farm, and finding it filled with everlasting treasure. This captivating story twists and turns like fiction but all is real, factual, and historical. This will be required reading for all students to grasp the impact and importance of our interwoven history, and serendipitous connections all the while, changing hearts towards kindness.

TOMMY DYO
Asian American Pacific Islander Community Advocate
National Director, Epic Movement

In Janice Munemitsu's new book, *The Kindness of Color*, she shares with us the difficulties and redemption of one Japanese American family during the internment period of WWII. She skillfully weaves in the kindness of color of a Hispanic family, a White banker, and a Jewish lawyer who was the son of Russian immigrants, as well as her own family. She shares how the kindness of different people was a factor not only for her family but the other families as well. How through the difficulty of internment of the Japanese Americans, the legacy of her family includes being connected to descendants of other family players in this beautiful saga. A must-read for those who are genuinely interested in breaking past the color barriers of our society to authentically see the goodness and kindness in the people around us.

GREG CAMPBELL
Management and Leadership Consultant
Author of *The Surprising Power of The Coil*

As an Orange County native and daughter of first-generation Indian immigrants, the intertwined stories of the Munemitsu and Mendez families hold a special place in my heart. I am extremely passionate about *Mendez v. Westminster*, and I take every opportunity to learn about the case and remind myself how grateful I am for the education I receive today. *The Kindness of Color* gave me this opportunity and *much* more by not only relating the story of *Mendez v. Westminster* to the incarceration of the Munemitsu family, but also expertly integrating family and community anecdotes to create a fascinating narrative. I loved this book, and I know you will too!

JASMINE CHHABRIA
National History Day Finalist, 2018
Keynote Speaker on *Mendez v. Westminster*
Class of 2022, Northwood High School, Irvine, CA

Janice Munemitsu carries on the legacy of generosity and kindness passed down to her by her grandparents, parents, uncles, and aunts. In *The Kindness of Color*, Janice tells the story of her family and the Mendez family, and how their lives intersected in a series of historical events that changed California and the United States. The book shares stories of how people courageously crossed barriers and found common ground, even during times of intense division in our nation. By doing so they built better communities and better lives. Janice shows how ordinary people faced with profound hardship, like racism, segregation, and even unjust incarceration, can work together to assure that America puts its principles into practice in pursuit of liberty and justice for all. I highly recommend this book as a resource for hope and wholeness during our present times full of fear and foreboding.

JEFF HITTENBERGER, PHD
Chief Academic Officer, Orange County Department of Education

THE KINDNESS OF COLOR

cultivating
Kindness,
Janice

THE KINDNESS OF COLOR

THE STORY OF TWO FAMILIES AND *MENDEZ, ET AL. V. WESTMINSTER*, THE 1947 DESEGREGATION OF CALIFORNIA PUBLIC SCHOOLS

優しさ　LA AMABILIDAD　KINDNESS

JANICE MUNEMITSU
FOREWORD BY SYLVIA MENDEZ

Barbwire imprisoned.

War of bombs and racism.

Hands offer kindness.

Fences keep you out.

Fight for school for all children.

Hands offer kindness.

No more high fences.

No barbwire to imprison.

Cultivate kindness.

TABLE of CONTENTS

By Sylvia Mendez

I have shared the story of *Mendez, et al. v. Westminster*—the 1947 federal court case that led to the desegregation of California public schools—since my retirement from nursing in 1993. I travel the nation speaking at schools and events, and telling of the courage, perseverance, and kindness of those who helped to bring about this monumental change. Despite the fact that it set up the precedent for the desegregation of all California public schools and preceded the famous 1954 *Brown v. Board of Education* Supreme Court ruling by seven years, I have found that few have heard of the groundbreaking *Mendez* case and the families behind it.

My dedication to sharing this story not only stems from my deep passion for encouraging students—especially minority students—in their education and reminding them how much they matter, but also because it is my family's story, my story. You see, when I was eight years old, my two brothers, Gonzalo and Jerome, and I were denied enrollment at the Westminster School District's Seventeenth Street school because of our last name and the color of our skin. Enrollment at Seventeenth Street was reserved for "white" children and we are of Mexican and Puerto Rican ancestry. Instead we were told we would have to attend the "Mexican" school in the area. There it was assumed students couldn't speak English well and didn't have the intelligence for more advanced subjects such as science, math, history, and literature. My parents, who were later joined by four other Mexican American families, fought in court to right this injustice not only for their children, but *para todos los niños*—for all the children.

Yet the story you find here does not only belong to my family. The author of *The Kindness of Color*, my friend Janice, has diligently chronicled the unlikely story of both of our families and their interwoven journeys during the difficulty of 1940s America. Brought to life in these pages, you will find the whole story of *Mendez, et al. v. Westminster* and how two immigrant families with different heritages were inadvertently brought together by their separate battles with racism. Ahead, you will read about much difficulty, racial ignorance, and pain, but also of the incredible kindness, grace, and collaboration that kept our hopes for a better future alive. That hope still lives in me, and I pray this story awakens it in you. Yes, this is the story of my family, Janice's family, and our people, yet it is also a story of all people and the community we can be when we look beyond our differences to see the beauty within each and all of us.

Sylvia Mendez
Recipient, US Presidential Medal of Freedom 2011

CHAPTER 1

The Kindness of Color

I choose to believe that life is interesting. On any given day, I can meet new people and learn a lot of new things. On some days, some very special days, I meet new people and learn new things that make a real, unforgettable impact on me and others. This day in the fall of 2002 was one of those days.

Like many people, I don't usually answer an unknown caller on my phone, as I assume it is just someone trying to sell me something. But for some reason, that day, I did pick up the call.

The voice on the other end was energetic and excited. "Hello, is this Janice Munemitsu?"

"Yes..." I began, skeptically. "Uh, who is this?"

"I'm Sandra Robbie and I'm producing a documentary about *Mendez v. Westminster*, the 1947 school desegregation case. Are you familiar with it? We are looking for the Munemitsu family that farmed in Westminster during World War II. Are you related to them?"

I was not familiar with the Mendez case, but Munemitsu, my family name, is an uncommon Japanese last name. "Yes, my dad and grandfather did farm in Westminster," I responded. I knew of the family farm, owned and worked by my family in the 1940s and '50s, but I wondered what it had to do with school desegregation. "Why are you looking for us?" I asked, as my curiosity grew.

And, when she answered, my part of this story began.

. . . .

My friendship with Sylvia Mendez also began right after that call. Sandra Robbie invited me to her interview shoot for the *Mendez, et al. v. Westminster* documentary just to meet the Mendez family. The eldest Mendez sister, Sylvia, wanted to reconnect with the Japanese American family that owned the farm where she lived at the time of the case. I knew *someone* had leased the farm from my father during those WWII years, but I had no idea of the bigger story and reunion that awaited me. When I met Sylvia Mendez and her brothers Gonzalo and Jerome for the first time, it felt like I was meeting part of my family that I never knew existed. I quickly realized that they remembered more about the details of my family's farm in Westminster than I had ever known. Meeting the Mendez family drew me into an adventure back in time, an opportunity to discover a far richer story than I could have ever imagined.

Since that day, I uncovered the story of how my family's history aligned, for a few short years, with that of the Mendez family. What I discovered of that shared story is recorded here. I am still amazed at how what I thought of as lost and insignificant family history now brings tears to the eyes of so many, inspires hope in others, and encourages people to persevere in the midst of seemingly insurmountable odds.

Once, after Sylvia and I shared our story with a group of educators, a young woman came up to me in tears. "I can't believe it," she said. "This story gives me hope." She told me about how she was at risk because of the threats that DACA (Deferred Action for Childhood Arrivals) young adults would be deported. Never mind that she had lived in the United States all her life, arriving as a young child with her parents. And though not a born-citizen, she had been educated in California and was now thriving as a responsible educator herself. Though the threat of deportation of DACA young adults was repealed in 2020, at that time her future was unknown.

The best I could do that day was to say, "There is always so much that is outside of our control, but hold onto hope, work hard, and do what you were created to do. Teach your children well, and I believe, no matter what, your story will be redeemed. It might not be easy. It might not be quick, but don't give up hope."

As she wiped away the tears, I hugged her warmly and she smiled with renewed hope for justice to be well served. If Sylvia's and my family's stories can inspire her to have hope that racism can be thwarted and eventually ended, then it is with the same hope that I share this story, *our* story, with you. A story of two families, hard work, community and—though difficult to see at times—hope for justice and a future.

. . . .

"Janice, Janice!" Someone was excitedly calling my name. The Sunday service at church had just ended and as I walked out, I saw my friend Joe waving and walking quickly toward me. He was very excited about something!

"Hi, what's up? How are you, Joe?" I asked.

"I saw you on TV last night!"

"Oh, you saw the Mendez documentary on PBS..." I felt embarrassed. Sandra Robbie's documentary, *Mendez vs. Westminster: Para Todos los Niños*, had just started airing and, despite the fact that it contained only a very short clip of me, I was getting recognized quite often.

Joe spoke rapidly, with great excitement, "*Yes*! I couldn't believe that story! About how Mr. Mendez and the other families fought for their kids to go to the regular public school. And not just for their kids, but for all the kids of California. It was amazing and it happened right here in Orange County! I didn't know that history at all. This story needs to be told. And do you know Sylvia, the girl who was banned from the white school? And what about her brothers? This story needs to be told so everyone knows about it."

"Yes, Sylvia and her brothers are great!" I enthusiastically replied, now riffing off his energy. "I just met them for the first time a few years ago. Gonzalo Jr. calls me his 'Japanese sister,' so I call him 'my Mexican brother'! They are a wonderful family and—"

Joe interrupted me mid-sentence, "And all those other families throughout Orange County—not just Westminster, but in Garden Grove, Santa Ana, and El Modena too! And now all kids of color go to public schools! I *just* didn't know, I didn't know..." His voice crackled and big tears rolled down his cheeks.

"Joe, are you okay?" I asked, concerned.

Joe looked at me, eye to eye, and said, through tears and a breaking voice, "It wasn't just *us*."

You see, Joe is Black and in 2006 he was probably in his early seventies. He had lived in California for many years, working and raising his family. But as a child who grew up in the American South, Joe had been a victim of racism, prejudice, and judgment because of the color of his skin.

"It wasn't just *us*." No, Joe, it wasn't just you as a Black man in America, but certainly over four hundred years of overt racism against Black citizens is among the worst injustices in US history—next to that of the persecution of Native American tribes.

As Joe and I talked, he told me how significant it was for him to know the local history of racism in California, the place that had been a safe haven to raise his family. (Or, at least, that had been safer than the South, where he had grown up as a child.) The fact that other races endured prejudice and bigotry in California was news to Joe and made him feel less alone in the fight for equality.

Shortly after our conversation, Joe moved back to Louisiana to retire on his family's farm. We lost touch after that and, given all the years that have gone by, Joe may have now passed to his heavenly home. But I will not forget the look on his face, the crackle in his voice, and his tears, when he said, "It wasn't just *us.*"

Joe's comment to me made me realize that this story is not just one about education in California during the 1920s through 1950s. This is not just a story of a Mexican cantina owner or a Japanese farmer. This is a story that other minorities in the US can relate to also. Sadly, racism still exists in our country. Many Black, Native American, Latino, and Asian people in America—along with other minority and non-English-speaking immigrant families—continue to experience its pain as innocent victims. Every act of racism is tragic and traumatizing to the victims. Every system and policy that props up racism and racist ideas in our country is unjust. Racism is a horrific part of history that should challenge us to work for lasting change so we can truly become the *land of the free.*

As a child, I said the Pledge of Allegiance every day at school. "I pledge allegiance to the Flag of the United States of America, and to the Republic for which it stands, one Nation under God, indivisible, with liberty and justice for all." This story is about *one nation under God* with the aspirational goals of being *indivisible, with liberty and justice for all.* These words, *liberty and justice for all,* are what we as Americans must strive towards if true change is to take root.

As I have shared both Sylvia's and my family's stories over the years, I have realized a powerful truth: kindness made all the difference for our families. *Kind* as an adjective is defined as the quality of being sympathetic, having a helpful and gentle nature, with the intent to give pleasure or bring relief to another.[1] I believe kindness also includes being generous, thoughtful, respectful, humble, and compassionate.

Neighbors, friends, and even strangers met the Mendez and Munemitsu families with kindness while we were in the midst of immense challenges. Each small act of kindness brought hope— hope that things could be different. No single person alone could upend the deeply rooted racism our families faced, but the kindness of many proved to unite a community and bring about true, lasting change.

As you read on, look for the qualities of kindness expressed by the many people of diverse backgrounds in the face of difficult, unfair, and unjust situations throughout this story. Amidst the challenges our families faced, kindness brought hope for the future and made a lasting difference. Kindness was expressed in many different ways by many different people, and most beautifully, by people of all colors to one another. I hope this story will encourage you, as much as it has me, to believe in the power of *The Kindness of Color.*

· · · · · · · · · · ·

Author's Note on Terminology

For this story, I will be respecting the terms commonly used by the different ethnic people I spoke to as they described themselves to me. The word *Mexican* was used by Sylvia in the sharing of her story and it was also used throughout the litigation to describe her family and others of Mexican descent, regardless of birthplace. *Mexican American* will also be used to designate heritage for those of Mexican descent born in the US. Expressions like *Chicano, Chicana, Latino, Latina,* and *Latinx* show the evolution

---

1 "Kind," *Merriam-Webster Online Dictionary.*

of terms over the years, but were not used in the mid-twentieth century. I will use *Black* for people of African American descent, *White* for people of Caucasian or European descent, and *Japanese* or *Japanese American* for those of Japanese ancestry.

CHAPTER 2

Getting to Know the Mendez Family

Sylvia Mendez has been my friend for nearly two decades now. But before getting that call from Sandra Robbie, all I knew was that my father had leased the farm he owned in Westminster, California, to someone during World War II. Now I know that "someone" to be Mr. and Mrs. Gonzalo and Felicitas Mendez from Santa Ana—Sylvia's parents.

Gonzalo Mendez Sr. was a sharp businessman, and as a young boy he was a bright and intelligent student. He was born in Chihuahua, Mexico, in 1913, and his family emigrated to California in 1919, when Gonzalo was seven. They settled in Westminster, where Gonzalo's aunt was already living, bought land, and began farming with money they had saved in Mexico. The local Westminster public school, Seventeenth Street School, was nearby, but all the Mexican children had to go to Hoover School, called the "Mexican school" by those who knew it. This was due to the school districts of Orange County segregating the White children from the Mexican children.

Earlier, during Mexico's Revolution (which lasted from 1910 to 1920, and moved the country from a dictatorship to a constitutional republic), many Mexicans immigrated to the southwestern United States, where most of them worked as field laborers. This mass migration caused Americans to fear the presumed non-English speakers and to look at them as the "other." From this fear, prejudice against Mexicans arose. In addition, the presumption that most of the Mexicans had poor English language skills was taken as a warrant to establish separate educational facilities and schools.

Felicitas and Gonzalo Mendez.
Courtesy of the Mendez family.

Newly settled in the United States, Gonzalo attended Hoover School, but he and three of his friends were quickly transferred to Seventeenth Street School, as they excelled in their classwork and needed academic challenge beyond what Hoover could provide.

Gonzalo loved school, but sadly, he had to leave the fifth grade to go work on the farm, as the family's situation changed drastically when his mother lost all the money they had. No longer was Gonzalo able to spend time in the books that he loved to study; instead, he had to trade them in for working long hours on the farm. Every day, he wished he could be at school. His older brother went on to Bible college in Azusa and got a job. But Gonzalo, as the younger brother, felt stuck on the farm and didn't have the opportunity to further his education. He so wished he could have completed school and gone to college.

Though Gonzalo would have preferred to continue his education instead of working in the fields, it was in the fields where he met Felipe Gomez. Felipe migrated with his family to the mainland from Puerto Rico in 1926. The Gomez family first moved to Arizona to pick cotton, but the working conditions were so terrible that they moved to California after just six months. After settling in Westminster, Felipe befriended Gonzalo and kindly invited him to his home, an act of hospitality that would change Gonzalo's life. Gonzalo met Felipe's beautiful daughter, Felicitas, whom he eventually married in 1935. At the time, Gonzalo was twenty-three years old, and Felicitas was twenty.

Felicitas was born in Juncos, Puerto Rico, in 1916. She was twelve years old when her family moved to Southern California from Arizona. Despite the fact that Puerto Ricans have been US citizens since 1917, upon their move to the mainland, the Gomez family was racially classified as "Mexican." (In 1898, following the Spanish-American War, the United States acquired Puerto Rico from Spain and it remains an unincorporated territorial possession to this day.)

After their wedding, Gonzalo and Felicitas worked together in the fields for three years, saving enough to open their own business. By their mid-twenties, Gonzalo and Felicitas had moved to Santa Ana and opened The Arizona Cantina, which served hungry customers with great food and friendly service. Both Felicitas and Gonzalo shared a strong work ethic and an entrepreneurial spirit for business. From the profits of The Arizona, they were able to purchase three houses. Meanwhile, they leased the space for their thriving cantina restaurant along a busy street in Santa Ana.

Gonzalo Sr. and Felicitas had a good life in Santa Ana in the 1930s, despite the aftermath of the Great Depression. They ran a busy and successful restaurant, where people would enjoy a good meal and linger to mingle with neighbors. By that time, they also had three children: Sylvia, Gonzalo Jr, and Jerome ("Jerry" as he was fondly called). Years later, another sister, Sandra, and brother, Phillip, were born. Gonzalo and Felicitas owned the big, white, wood house on the corner of Third Street and Raitt, as well as two smaller houses they rented out. Sylvia, born in 1936, loved living in that big house in Santa Ana and recalls its three bedrooms well: the front bedroom for her parents, the middle bedroom for her, and the back bedroom shared by her two brothers.

Felicitas and Gonzalo Mendez with daughter Sylvia
and son Gonzalo Jr. in the late 1930s.
Courtesy of the Mendez family.

Gonzalo was well-known in the Santa Ana community, going flying with White and Mexican business friends who were pilots and hosting neighborly poker parties at home. Race wasn't a sticking point for him among his Santa Ana entrepreneur friends at the time. Gonzalo applied for citizenship and proudly became a US citizen at age thirty. Now, after working in the fields and having become the owner of his own business, he could truly call California his "home."

Among Gonzalo's business relationships was his friendship with Mr. Frank Monroe, who worked at First Western Bank of Garden Grove. I'm not sure why Gonzalo banked in Garden Grove and not Santa Ana. It may have something to do with the fact that in the 1930s and 1940s, Orange County was mostly rural farm land, and there wasn't a bank on every block. Furthermore, Mr. Monroe, a White man born in Texas, didn't discriminate against those who were not White. This was far from a guarantee in the 1930s. He valued his customers, regardless of their ethnic heritage, and respected them as friends and neighbors in the community.

This was so true that, every weekday, Mr. Monroe would visit Gonzalo at The Arizona to collect that day's revenue in order to deposit the money in the Mendez bank account. That way Gonzalo didn't have to leave the cantina during business hours. These visits strengthened not only their banking relationship, but also their friendship and trust over the years.

Kindness is...going out of your way to help a friend.

As an adult, driven by his love for study and learning, Gonzalo had become a successful entrepreneur, and it was that same love that shaped how he felt about education for his own children.

Being unable to finish his own formal education fueled his passion to make sure his children did finish theirs. And eventually it would be these seeds, planted in Gonzalo as a young boy, that would grow in him the resolve to fight for all Mexican children in California to receive the same public-school education that the White children did.

. . . .

Growing up in Santa Ana made for a wonderful childhood for the Mendez children. Sylvia, Gonzalo and Felicitas' eldest, recalls all the fun she had growing up with the neighborhood children in the Santa Ana "barrio." *Barrio* is defined as (1) a ward, quarter, or district of a city or town in a Spanish-speaking country, or (2) a Spanish-speaking quarter or neighborhood in a city or town in the US, especially in the Southwest.[2] During Sylvia's childhood, the barrio in question was a cultural and majority-language designation of an area of Spanish-speaking Santa Ana.

Unfortunately, in more recent times, *barrio* has been used as a slight towards Spanish-speaking neighborhoods, implying that they are low-income and high-crime areas. But when Sylvia and her brothers were growing up, the Santa Ana barrio was a thriving area of Mexican culture and bilingual Spanish- and English-speaking neighbors. All the barrio neighborhood children would walk to Fremont Elementary School for their education. It was about five or six blocks for Sylvia and her brothers. Fremont School was right on the border of the neighborhood district and was known as the school for "Mexican" children.

In the 1930s and 1940s, the Santa Ana School District was segregated by district borders, i.e., the schools were located in neighborhoods with district boundaries determining which school a child would attend. The Mendez children attended the

2 "Barrio," *Merriam-Webster Online Dictionary.*

Fremont School, because the district lines were drawn at Artesia Street (now known as Raitt Street). Franklin School, the all-White school, was only a block away from the Mendez home in the opposite direction of Fremont. However, the school district boundary line was drawn right at their block.

Sylvia, Gonzalo Jr. (back), and Jerome (front) Mendez
with their babysitter (unidentified) around 1940.
Courtesy of the Mendez family.

School segregation existed in Santa Ana, but it was masked by basing the existing district boundary lines on residential neighborhoods. This type of "de facto" segregation existed, but because of the community and all the children going to the schools designated by the school district boundary lines, it was generally accepted despite the underlying neighborhood separation and prejudice. It was not based on any individual bias by the registration process at any given school by any given school registrar.

Despite this segregation, the education at Fremont School where children from the barrio attended was not noticeably inferior to the education at Franklin School, where the mostly White children attended. Most students at Fremont were bilingual, but some were children of new immigrants who spoke little English. Sylvia remembers that her principal, Miss Gilbert, found creative, nondiscriminatory ways to help the Spanish-speaking students with English. One of the things she did was teach the children to all sing popular songs in English. This was a great way to start class and an innovative way for Miss Gilbert to teach the students English and about the American culture of the day.

Sylvia spoke English well and loved singing the songs as they all started class together. In many ways, Miss Gilbert was building comradery and community between the students who already spoke English and those who were just learning English by giving them unifying songs to sing. She was not trying to segregate out students, but welcome them by singing together at the start of each day of school.

Kindness is...being unifying and inclusive.

Many California public services and areas were segregated during this time. For example, public swimming pools were segregated and limited Mexicans to only Mondays, the day the pool would be drained and cleaned at night. Orange County was no different than other areas of California, the West Coast, and the rest of the US. By 1930, there were about fifteen "Mexican" schools in the county that were below acceptable safety and educational standards. Fire hazards, electric fences, poor lighting, inadequate ventilation, and untrained or poorly resourced teachers were common in these schools.

The school districts of Westminster, Garden Grove, El Modena, Santa Ana, Anaheim, Orange, Placentia, La Habra, and Costa Mesa all had separate "Mexican" schools. Santa Ana had the Fremont School and Franklin. El Modena designated Lincoln as the "Mexican" school and Roosevelt as the White. In Garden Grove, Mexican children attended Hoover School, while White children attended Lincoln Elementary. And in Westminster, Hoover was for Mexican students and Seventeenth Street was for White students. Though there were separate schools for Mexican children, in California it was up to the individual local school districts as to whether other non-White children (those of African, Asian, or Native American descent) would be allowed to go to the White schools.

It is important for us to understand that this discrimination was not something that just arose out of nowhere. Rather it had deep roots in the history of our land.

CHAPTER 3

This Land Is Your Land...
Or Is It?

American folk singer Woody Guthrie wrote the lyrics to a popular American folk song, "This Land Is Your Land." Originally written in 1940, the song was intended by Guthrie as a protest against the economic inequalities that existed at the time, and the suffering of millions during the Great Depression. The lyrics insisted that this land was made for all—for you and for me—a lifelong mantra of Guthrie and a call for social justice.[3]

But the question is, have Americans and the US government stewarded the land and opportunities as their constitutional amendments and Bill of Rights intended: for *all*? The roots of school segregation and the Japanese American "internment" go far deeper than 1940s school districts or World War II.

Native Americans were the first people indigenous to the area now known as California. Tribes were mostly nomadic within a given geographic area, hunting and gathering food from the vast natural resources of the land. Some historical theories suggest Native Americans migrated by walking over a (now ocean-covered) land bridge from Asia to North America. However, new evidence is being unearthed that these early peoples in North

---

3 Eighty years later, on January 20, 2021, the inauguration of President Joe Biden as the forty-sixth president of the United States included Jennifer Lopez performing "This Land Is Your Land" as part of a medley that featured "America the Beautiful."

and South America actually came by sea from Asia or Pacific Oceana. Whatever their route, these Native Americans were the first inhabitants of our land and courageous explorers in their own right.

In the mid-1550s, European explorers came to hunt and seek those same natural resources for trade purposes, though they did not attempt to colonize the area at first. After all, the area known today as California was difficult to reach and very isolated from trade routes, making it unattractive for European colonization. Some came by ship across the Pacific Ocean, trying to circumnavigate the globe, while others sailed all the way around the tip of South America, Cape Horn. Either way, the vastness of the Pacific Ocean and its strong currents made the voyage treacherous, and numerous ships and sailors were lost in the journey.

Beginning in the mid-1700s, the Spanish, in control of Mexico, were the first to set their sights on colonizing Alta (or upper) California, north of Spanish-controlled Baja (lower) California. The Spanish efforts testified to a desire for military control of the land while Franciscan friars led by Father Junipero Serra were passionate to evangelize—to bring Christianity to the Native American tribes in California. Twenty-one California missions were founded along the California coast between 1769-1823, from the first, Mission San Diego de Alcalá in the south, to the last, Mission San Francisco Solano, north of San Francisco in Sonoma, California.

The true intention of Spain, however, was control of an important coastline and land acquisition. The Spanish Empire wanted to gain this control through Spanish European conquest of what we now know as the California coast. The empire was driven by the military and political advantages control of the coast would bring, the potential of fertile inland valleys that could be cultivated, and the use of the missions to colonize and culturally assimilate the native tribes. The ultimate goal was to conquer the territory as a colony for Spain and extract the wealth of the land. Sadly, with their conquest, they also brought disease to the native tribes, which killed off a large percentage of the population.

Each mission was set up with a central mission church as well as housing for the priests, Native American converts to Christianity, and military soldiers. They also included vast agricultural farms with herds of cattle and other livestock, and trading outposts. Spanish military forces also built several forts (presidios) and three small towns (pueblos) along the Alta California coast. The cities of Los Angeles and San Jose had humble beginnings as two of the original towns known as pueblos. In what is now Orange County, California, the ninth mission, Mission San Juan Capistrano, established in 1776, had a peak population of over 1,361 Native Americans in 1812. By 1819, the mission had over fourteen thousand head of cattle and sixteen thousand sheep.[4]

Mexico won independence from Spain in 1821, took control of Alta California, and subsequently, the Mexican government closed the missions and nationalized the church properties. As the mission era ended, white Hispanics of Spanish descent, known as *Californios*, controlled the land grants over the vast mission rancho system throughout California.

A dispute over the border between Texas and Mexico erupted into the Mexican American War, which was fought between 1846 and 1848. The war was formally ended when the 1848 Treaty of Guadalupe Hidalgo was signed. The United States paid Mexico $15 million in exchange for the disputed Texas territory, as well as the land which is now the states of New Mexico, Arizona, Utah, Nevada, parts of Colorado, and all of Alta California. This was an unbelievably large sum of money in the mid-1850s, and it was

---

4 McLaughlin, *The California Missions Source Book*, 34-35.

spent in order to acquire a continuous coast-to-coast territory. The purchased land was open, wild, and unpopulated, with large portions of desert wasteland. Probably, to Mexico, it seemed a good deal at the time. California became a territory of the United States in 1848. Little did they know the value that lay hidden in the California dirt.

News travelled slowly without modern communication like cell phones and the internet, so when gold was discovered at Sutter's Mill, Coloma, California, just nine days before the Treaty of Guadalupe Hidalgo was signed, this news wasn't known nationally for days, maybe weeks. When the news got out, it was too late for Mexico to back out of the deal. The Gold Rush of 1849 was on and thousands of "forty-niners" came from all over the world to seek their fortune, panning for California gold as California's population quickly grew to over 250,000. An estimated 750,000 pounds of gold was found, worth approximately $2,000,000,000.[5] Only a few of the tens of thousands of gold seekers became rich, but California had become the Golden State.

The Gold Rush of 1849 was a motivating factor for California's quick acquirement of statehood after only two years as a US territory. When applying for statehood, California's proposed constitution barred the Southern system of racial slavery, which provoked debate in Congress between pro-slavery and anti-slavery politicians. Congress debated and finally accepted California as a free, non-slavery state, and as the thirty-first state of the United States, on September 9, 1850.

If its residents didn't strike it rich with gold, California still offered them opportunities in agriculture and work building the infrastructure. These opportunities were especially attractive to immigrants fleeing poverty in their own countries. Many

5 "8 Things You May Not Know About the California Gold Rush," https://www.history.com/news/8-things-you-may-not-know-about-the-california-gold-rush.

immigrants from China were recruited by railroad companies to do heavy manual labor on a railroad destined to span from coast to coast. In 1869, the Transcontinental Railroad was finished, connecting Council Bluffs, Iowa, to the San Francisco Bay.

Beginning in 1852, competition for jobs fueled ongoing conflict and discrimination between Chinese and Whites, eventually leading to the Chinese Exclusion Act of 1882. Signed by President Chester Arthur in 1882, this act suspended Chinese immigration and declared Chinese immigrants ineligible for naturalization, the process whereby US citizenship is granted to a lawful permanent resident after he or she meets the Immigration and Nationality Act requirements. Additional California legislation in the Geary Act of 1892 extended the ban on Chinese immigration for another ten years, until 1902. The Supreme Court further ruled in 1902 that Chinese immigration was banned, and this ban held until the Magnuson Act of 1943 allowed Chinese immigration for the first time since 1882.[6]

It was not only the Chinese that were discriminated against by being barred from entering the US. The Immigration Act of 1924 signed by President Coolidge was fueled by the American desire to stop the influx of hardworking, but largely unskilled, non-English-speaking immigrants looking for jobs and opportunity. While this act greatly limited immigrants from Southern and Eastern Europe, it also no longer allowed Japanese immigrants to be admitted to the United States.[7]

California still needed large numbers of workers to work in the fields, and by the mid-1920s, Mexicans made up 75 percent of all California farm workers. Philippa Strum writes, "The agribusinesses then turned to Mexicans as a labor supply. They

6 Chinese Exclusion Act, https://www.history.com/topics/immigration/chinese-exclusion-act-1882.

7 Immigration Act of 1924, https://www.history.com/this-day-in-history/coolidge-signs-stringent-immigration-law.

were not interested in recruiting new citizens; rather, they were determined to maintain a cheap labor supply, and their disdain for their workers was obvious in the way they treated the new arrivals. Mexican workers who remained permanently in the United States would face the same kind of contempt and discrimination that had been meted out to the Chinese and Japanese."[8]

While the Californios of "White Hispanic" ancestry, who had lived in California from its early founding, integrated into the growing majority White culture, the darker-skinned Mexican laborers came to California out of economic necessity, with hopes of finding work and making a meager living. As their families came, many lived in poorer neighborhoods and worked hard to establish themselves in a new culture and country. Living conditions were poor for most and their health was often compromised because of illness and disease like tuberculosis. While the Mexican immigrants had a strong community among themselves, they were seen by the White majority as "others" and unfairly judged to be of lower intelligence because of language barriers and cultural differences.

These unfair stereotypes, and fear of competition for jobs, resulted in the US Census Bureau announcing in 1930 that "Mexican" was denoted as a separate race. Mexicans were now defined as people born in Mexico or born in the United States to Mexican parents who were not "definitely white, Negro, Indian [Native American], Chinese or Japanese."[9] Mexicans living in the US had long considered themselves to be of Spanish European descent and therefore, "white." The Mexican government was outraged by the Census Bureau's change and, under political pressure, the Census Bureau agreed to drop the category. The 1940 census reclassified Mexicans as white if they were not "definitely

8 Strum, *Mendez v. Westminster*, 6.
9 Strum, *Mendez v. Westminster*, 9.

Indian or of other nonwhite race." Strum notes, "In a society that created the phenomenon of racial categories and then judged people according to where they fit into them, the Mexicans could take whatever comfort they might choose in their classification as part of the dominant race."[10]

During the Great Depression, almost 25 percent of all Americans were out of jobs and this led many White Americans to accuse hardworking immigrants of all races of taking their work opportunities and livelihoods. In 1931, President Herbert Hoover authorized a deportation of "aliens," which resulted in more than 365,000 Mexicans and Mexican American citizens to be repatriated to Mexico between 1929 and 1932. In Orange County, California, alone, nearly two thousand "Mexicans" returned to Mexico.[11]

This is the context in which public school segregation against children of color came to be. The prevailing prejudice and bias against immigrants was in conflict with the government's constitutional obligation to educate all children. California enacted several laws that show the progression of segregation in schools. In 1855, California law required the state's school funds to "be apportioned to counties on the basis of a census of white children, ages 4 to 18." In 1860, another state law "prohibited colored children from attending integrated schools but permitted school districts to operate separate schools, if they chose to do so, for Blacks, Indians, and Asians."[12] California entered the Union as a "free" state against slavery, yet that did not ensure equality for its residents or equal schooling for all the children.

The establishment of "Mexican" schools began in the early 1900s throughout Southern California. By the mid-1920s, Orange

---

10 Strum, *Mendez v. Westminster*, 10.

11 Strum, *Mendez v. Westminster*, 10.

12 Strum, *Mendez v. Westminster*, 13.

County had the fifteen "Mexican" schools listed earlier, mostly located close to the farming areas where the Mexican families worked and lived. The separate schools were weakly justified by the (often false) idea that Mexican children did not have a suitable understanding of English and were underperforming students. School districts viewed the segregation as appropriate, claiming fears of Mexican students falling far behind the White students. They, however, didn't make exceptions for Mexican students who spoke English well and could meet the academic challenges of the White schools. The school administrators clearly believed that Mexican students were inferior intellectually to White students.

Children of the White Hispanic Californios, who came from more prosperous families, were allowed to attend White schools. The Californios children performed just as well academically as the other White children did. Yet the darker and generally more impoverished children of the same race and ethnic heritage were excluded because of their language and culture. All the while, school district administrators held to their belief and prejudice that Mexican American students had inferior intellectual and academic ability, therefore justifying their separate "Mexican" schools.

By 1934, 25 percent of Orange County's total student enrollment—roughly four thousand students—was made up of Mexican or Mexican American children.[13] And 40 percent of the county's Mexican students lived in these four school district areas: Westminster, Garden Grove, El Modena, and Santa Ana. And of those students, the vast majority attended a "Mexican" school.

This sets the scene and is the history that would provide the fuel for those seeking justice. School segregation was wrong and needed to be corrected. But how, when, and who would take

---

13 Strum, *Mendez v. Westminster*, 19-20.

a stand? History would find its answer when the unexpected relocation of the Mendez family took them from Santa Ana city living to rural Westminster farm life.

To a farm owned by the Munemitsu family.

CHAPTER 4

From Japan to California

Just as Gonzalo came with his family to Westminster from Mexico, my grandfather had come to the US from Japan, and he was already farming in Southern California in the 1920s. My grandfather Seima Munemitsu was born in Kochi-ken, Shikoku, Japan in 1899. His father, my great-grandfather, Fusakichi Munemitsu, immigrated by ship to the US in the early 1900s, working as a farm laborer. In 1914, Fusakichi's wife, Fugio, immigrated to the US, followed by his son Seima in 1916. Seima was seventeen years old and, upon his arrival, began working as a farm laborer alongside his father.

This was in the midst of World War I (which lasted from 1914 to 1918) and both Fusakichi and his son Seima registered for the WWI draft as US residents. Neither were called to serve, but, even as new immigrant residents, they would have fought for their new homeland if they had been called. During World War I, they both continued as farm laborers on the Carson Ranch in Torrance, California.

Sadly, in 1921, Seima's mother, Fugio, died at the young age of forty-two, likely of heart disease. Seima, now twenty-one, left California to court his future bride, returning by ship to Kochi-ken. He married Masako Morioka, age seventeen, also from Kochi. Returning to California, the newlyweds arrived in San Francisco in 1921 to begin their life together.

Seima (in a western-style suit) and Masako (in her traditional kimono)
Munemitsu as newlyweds in 1921, the year they came to California.

Seima and Masako had their first son, my father, Seiko Lincoln "Tad" Munemitsu, the following year, 1922. Seiko was born in Torrance, California—a first-generation American citizen and a second-generation Japanese American. Imagine two new immigrants from Japan naming their son "Lincoln" after President Abraham Lincoln! What a tangible way to show their eagerness to be part of the American story, with hopes of freedom and opportunity! My dad was born on February 13, a day after President Lincoln's birthday and the day before Valentine's Day. My dad always said he was grateful that his parents chose "Lincoln," not "Valentine," for his middle name. A year later in 1923, they had another son, Saylo, and twelve years later in 1935, twin daughters, Akiko and Kazuko.

As Japanese immigrants, it was clear that Seima and Masako wanted to enculturate into American life. Seima was "Pops" to his kids and Masako was "Mom," forgoing the Japanese words for father (*otosan*) and mother (*okaasan*).

No one remembers for sure how it began, but Seiko's lifelong nickname was "Tad." His mother called him *Tadao*, making a Japanese name out of *Tad*. Tad himself said it was short for "tadpole." But for a man who wasn't scared of many things, Tad sure didn't like frogs. Interestingly, President Abraham Lincoln's son was also called "Tad," and perhaps that was what led to this Japanese American schoolboy using the name. However he got it, it became his lifelong first name and, throughout his life, few even knew him as Seiko Lincoln.

Masako and sons, Tad and Saylo, in the mid-1920s.

My dad and his siblings were considered *Nisei*, or second-generation Japanese Americans. Most other cultures just say they are first, second, third generation, but in Japanese, the terms are *Issei, Nisei, Sansei*, and so on. These terms are not just used as descriptors: in Japanese culture, these words carry more identity than that. My grandparents Seima and Masako were first-generation Japanese immigrants and first-generation American residents, so they are considered Issei. The second generation (my father and his siblings) are called Nisei, and are born here in the States. I am Sansei, the third generation born in the US.

Typically, the Issei spoke a little English, and had Japanese as their primary language. Nisei were the language and cultural bridge, speaking Japanese to parents and English in school, business, college, etc. Sansei speak mostly English, with little-to-some Japanese, but usually by the third generation, Sansei are raised quite American. *Yonsei* would be the fourth generation and they are most likely fully enculturated into the American lifestyle and English language, sometimes with very little knowledge of their Japanese heritage, depending on their family of origin.

. . . .

In 1931, Seima and Masako, with their two sons, moved from Torrance, California, to Westminster, California, to farm. At first, Seima leased land to farm. Land ownership for the Munemitsus only became a possibility because of the kindness of the widow who owned the land that they were farming. At her death, her final will gave her tenants, Seima and Tad, the "first right of refusal." This gave them the opportunity to finally purchase her farmland, and this was the chance Seima had been waiting for.

Kindness is...giving immigrants opportunities
they would not normally have.

Due to their hard-earned savings, the Munemitsus were ready to make the purchase. Unfortunately, Seima couldn't rightfully own the land because of the California Alien Land Law of 1913, which "prohibited the ownership of agricultural land" by "aliens ineligible to citizenship." Seima did not have citizenship.

Instead, a trusted Nisei friend, a US citizen born in Hawaii, stepped in as an adult guardian for Tad, making the purchase legal and listing Seima's young son—a US citizen—as the owner of the farm. This began Tad's experience as head of the family farm, as well as his experience of the significant responsibility that came with that. Tad's sister, my aunt Aki (short for Akiko) says that Tad went to the bank as a young boy of eight years old to translate English to Japanese for their father. No doubt, this was also the beginning of young Tad's business and banking education, which served him well as the farm's owner throughout the rest of his life.

Tad and Saylo in work overalls with Masako, Namio, and Sam Munemitsu on the Westminster farm. Namio was Seima's stepmother and Sam his young stepbrother.

The Munemitsu farm was on Edwards Street in Westminster, back when the city was mostly farmland and small neighborhoods. It was forty acres with a farmhouse, four workers' cottages, a packing house, and a barn. The modest family farmhouse had a kitchen but it didn't have indoor plumbing, so instead there were two outhouses: one for the residents of the family house, and one for the residents of the four workers' cottages.

Seima made big wooden *ofuro*: Japanese-style bathtubs, one each in two adjacent bathhouses. Each tub was about four feet wide and three feet tall. I suspect he made these knowing how good a hot bath would feel after a hard day's work on the farm.

In addition to the family working the farm, there were fourteen *braceros* (Mexican laborers allowed into the US for a limited time as seasonal agricultural workers) who worked and lived in the four cottages on the property. Masako would cook meals in a second big kitchen built with a long dining table to feed the hungry bracero workers. She was a very good cook, especially when it came to making large quantities of food for family, friends, and workers. In addition to traditional Japanese food, I remember Masako, my grandmother, making the lightest, crispiest fried chicken ever. It was always a family favorite, and I believe she likely perfected her recipe in that kitchen after countless meals made for the hardworking farmhands!

My grandfather was a hardworking and very practical man. Perhaps because of his experience in the Great Depression, he used to say, "If you can't eat it, don't plant it." Vegetables like cabbage and asparagus were some of the main crops at that time. Asparagus was harvested when the tender shoots were about a foot long and about a quarter size in diameter. Then the asparagus was sized and packed in wood crates before being taken to the produce market in Los Angeles. In later years, our family would grow strawberries, green beans, tomatoes, and squash in Orange County.

Masako and Seima in front of their home on the Westminster farm.

•　•　•　•　•　•　•　•　•　•　•

As a young boy, my dad, Tad, was a victim of polio, a highly contagious, disabling, and life-threatening disease. There was a significant US epidemic in 1916 and polio continued to be a threat until a vaccine was developed for widespread use in the mid-1950s. Children were especially vulnerable as polio attacks the spinal cord and nervous system and, at its worst, results in paralysis, impaired breathing, and even death.

Tad suffered paralysis and deformity in his right foot that required specially fitted, high-top leather shoes that fit over his ankles. I remember that my dad basically had only one style of shoe, in two colors: his high-top, dusty, brown leather work boots to wear at the farm, and high-top, black, polished leather boots for nice occasions. While he never complained about the pain, I know that as a farmer on his feet all day, he wasn't pain-free. It was something he endured his whole life.

While Tad had the middle name Lincoln, after the sixteenth president of the United States, unfortunately, he was plagued with polio just like the thirty-second president, Franklin D. Roosevelt. Polio struck every class, race, and neighborhood of society, and in the summer of 1921, over a decade before he would become president, Roosevelt suffered polio at the age of thirty-nine, while he was assistant secretary of the Navy. Polio left Roosevelt paralyzed in both legs, fully reliant on a wheelchair for mobility. Photographs of him avoided showing him in his wheelchair and he used braces and canes to appear to walk. Despite his disability, Roosevelt was elected president of the United States, and he served from 1933 to 1945.[14]

One of the few pictures of FDR in a wheelchair was taken to raise funds for polio research. This led to the founding of the National Foundation for Infantile Paralysis in 1938—later known as the March of Dimes.[15]

His presidency had significant challenges, such as bringing a nation out of the Great Depression, leading the US through World War II, and facing the continuing threat of the same disease that had robbed him of his ability to walk. In a radio broadcast to raise funds to fight polio, Roosevelt said, "The dread disease that we battle at home, like the enemy we oppose abroad, shows no concern, no pity for the young. It strikes—with its most frequent and devastating force—against children. And that is why much of the future strength of America depends upon the success that we achieve in combating this disease."[16]

In 1952, a peak of over fifty-eight thousand polio cases were reported in the United States, with more than three thousand deaths. Successful vaccines became widely available by injection in 1955 (due to the research of Dr. Jonas Salk), and in an oral form

14 Franklin D. Roosevelt, https://www.history.com/topics/us-presidents/franklin-d-roosevelt.

15 March of Dimes, https://www.history.com/this-day-in-history/franklin-roosevelt-founds-march-of-dimes.

16 Franklin D. Roosevelt Pleads Victory Against Polio, 1/29/1944, https://www.historyofvaccines.org/content/fdr-pleads-victory-against-polio.

in 1962 (due to the work of Dr. Albert Sabin).[17] Since 1979, there have been no cases of polio in the US thanks to ongoing nation-wide vaccinations of babies and children. That Tad survived polio and persevered with the residual disability is thanks, in large measure, to his loving family.

· · · · · · · · · · · ·

My grandpa Seima had a big heart for children and invited two other boys to live with his family. While their parents went back to live in Japan (reason unknown), both Mamoru and Seimi stayed in California to live with the Munemitsu family. These boys would have many more opportunities in America than in Japan, and they quickly became part of the family. In old family photographs, it almost looks like there were four Munemitsu sons working, going to school, and playing together. This was the start of lifelong friendships for the boys.

Kindness is...caring for the children of others as your own and letting the lines between family and friends blur.

Together, Tad, Saylo, Mamoru, and Seimi attended Huntington Beach Unified High School, one of only nine high schools in Orange County at the time. This may be hard to believe now, as Orange County has gone from the farmland of Southern

---

17 Polio, https://www.history.com/
news/8-things-you-may-not-know-about-jonas-salk-and-the-polio-vaccine.

California to a highly populated urban and business center. In 2020, there were twenty-seven school districts, and sixty-three high schools in Orange County, with nearly five hundred thousand students attending Orange County public schools.

Typical all-American young men love cars: Saylo, friends Seimi and Mamoru, and Tad hanging out with beloved cars on the Westminster farm.

In the 1930s and 1940s, Orange County school districts did not restrict Japanese-Americans from attending the regular elementary, junior high, or high schools. This varied by area in California, as it was decided by individual school districts. Since there were so few high schools in Orange County at the time, there weren't many options to segregate high school students into separate schools by race.

Was there prejudice against the Japanese Americans when Tad went to school? Yes, discrimination was common and prejudice came in the form of insulting racial slurs and schoolyard fistfights. There were few Japanese families in Westminster at the time, so the school had mostly White students. The bullying included name-calling, fights, and whatever else some of the White boys could think of to torment Tad and his other Japanese American friends. My dad talked about being called offensive slang words and getting into fistfights because he was of Japanese heritage. Fortunately, these bullies were the minority and anti-Japanese racism was not actively supported by the school district, administration, the majority of the teachers, or the culture of the time.

Tad had many friends at school and was involved in track and field (even with his clubfoot from childhood polio), photography, and other school activities. His high school yearbooks are full of well wishes and fond memories of Huntington Beach High School "Oiler" friends. (The high school mascot name "Oilers" was due to the vast number of hammer-like oil derricks adjacent to the school buildings and field. In 1920, oil was discovered in Huntington Beach and the small farm community became an active and growing city.)

Neither polio nor prejudice stopped Tad from living a full life at school and home. However, these would prove to be only the first of many significant challenges this young Nisei farmer would face.

CHAPTER 5

The Kind of Friend Everyone Should Have: Mr. Frank Monroe

In the days when my father started farming, there were no credit or debit cards, and no ATMs. There was no such thing as online or electronic banking, because, well, "online" hadn't been invented yet! Bank customers had a small paper bank book where the deposits and the withdrawals were recorded by hand, even into the 1970s. The bank tellers made the entries in pen and wrote their initials next to each entry as authorization. You had to actually go into the bank, and wait your turn to deposit or withdraw money from your bank account.

Most banks also relied on their reputations of honesty and integrity. This was especially important because of the impact and ongoing effects of the Great Depression, the worst economic downturn in the history of the industrialized world, which lasted from 1929 to 1939. The Great Depression began after the stock market crash in October of 1929, which sent Wall Street into a panic and wiped out millions of investors. Local bank customers literally ran to take their money out of banks. Local banks didn't have enough cash in their vaults at any given time for everyone to make total withdrawals. Imagine having no money in a cash society without credit cards! Families suffered greatly during the

Great Depression, living as frugally as possible, and saving any extra money they could.

This was the context for the important relationships Frank Monroe of First Western Bank of Garden Grove had with not only Gonzalo Mendez, but also with Seima and Tad Munemitsu.

Mr. Monroe was the kind of friend and banker everyone should have. Not only did he work hard for his customers at the bank, but he got to know them personally, learning of their hopes and dreams for the future. This is why Mr. Monroe knew of not only Gonzalo's business success, but also of his lifelong dream of being the boss of his own farm. Gonzalo would tell him how much he hated being the mere farmworker in his youth, how he regretted not finishing his education to help his family, and how he really wanted to be a farmer.

Frank Monroe had also known the Munemitsu family as bank customers since Tad was just a young boy, probably starting around 1931, when the Munemitsus moved from Torrance to Westminster to farm. Mr. Monroe became a mentor to young Tad as he patiently helped him learn basic banking and business. I can imagine my dad, just a boy of about eight or nine years old, going to the bank with my grandpa, and translating English to Japanese for him. I'm sure Mr. Monroe spent a lot of time with them, patiently letting my dad translate for Grandpa, as well as taking the time to explain banking and business concepts to an eight-year-old! It's no wonder my dad grew in his knowledge of business, hands-on, without textbooks. He had a mighty fine teacher and mentor in Mr. Monroe. My dad would say Mr. Monroe was "about as honest a man as you can find. Very honest and sincere, with no prejudice towards us."

Kindness is...taking time to help others,
no matter how young they are.

My dad's connection to Mr. Monroe continued well beyond those early years. Every Christmas, I remember making visits to many of my parents' friends to take gifts. This always included a visit to Mrs. Enola Monroe. She was probably in her eighties when I was just a child. She lived in a lovely white house with green trim on Euclid Street in Garden Grove, just down the street from the First Western Bank where her husband worked. Her front yard had a white picket fence and her lawn was always a beautiful and healthy green. She had beautiful antique furniture and lace doilies with pretty china tea sets and dishes. At Christmas, she decorated her tree with delicate antique ornaments and silver tinsel.

One year on our way home, I got curious and asked, "How do we know Mrs. Monroe?" My dad simply replied, "Her husband was a good friend to me." It was decades later that I realized that Mr. Monroe was the banker who helped my grandpa and dad in the early years. There was a deep sense of loyalty and gratitude in these annual Christmas visits with Mrs. Monroe for my dad.

Growing up in the 1960s and 1970s, I also remember how much my dad and I loved watching *National Geographic* shows. It seemed our house had every edition of *National Geographic* magazine ever printed in full color—at least as a young girl, I thought so. I enjoyed every edition with its full color photographs, and some even included maps of countries, continents, and faraway places. They were delivered in the mail, with a brown paper wrap around each copy to protect the pages and cover. I remember wondering, "How did Dad get all these?"

As it turns out, Mr. Monroe had gifted my dad what he called "a lifetime subscription" to *National Geographic,* one of the few ways to see the world in those days before television and commercial airlines. No doubt, this fueled Dad's love of nature and the animal world in days when air travel was a true luxury and certainly out of our budget.

He continued to have a bank account at that bank location until his death in 1997 (despite the bank changing management many times through the decades). I don't think my dad could imagine not banking at the bank where he met his first business mentor and "hands-on" banking instructor. He was so grateful for, and never forgot the kindness of, his banker friend, even long after Mr. Monroe passed. The friendship of Mr. Monroe was lifelong and a great treasure to my dad. This relationship became especially important when future unforeseen challenges arose, requiring wisdom and guidance. Little did my twenty-year-old dad know that his whole world would change as World War II advanced.

Kindness is...remembering those who helped you with gratitude.

CHAPTER 6

World War II: When Crisis and Danger Present Opportunity?

World War II began in 1939 when German forces, led by the Nazi regime, invaded Poland. In response, France and Great Britain declared war on Germany to try to stop their invasion across Europe. Japan, who had made a political alliance with Germany, had been at war with China since 1937 in East Asia, and expanded their ambitions in the Pacific with an attack on United States soil at Pearl Harbor, Oahu, Hawaii, on December 7, 1941. The deadly attack killed 2,403 American civilians and military personnel.

Tad remembers that he was harvesting cabbage in the field on Sunday morning, December 7, 1941. It was before lunch and a man yelled ugly racial slurs out his car window as he drove by the Munemitsu farm. Not knowing what provoked this man's actions, Tad and his fellow workers continued their labors. When they stopped for lunch, one of the workers told him what he heard on the radio: imperial Japan had bombed Pearl Harbor! They all listened to the broadcast in shock, wondering what would happen next.

Little did Tad know the injustice he and his family were about to face.

The United States responded to the Pearl Harbor attack by

declaring war in the Pacific against Japan, and joining the Allied Forces in the fight in Europe. The two major global political alliances at that time were the Allied Forces and the Axis Powers. The Allied Forces of Great Britain, France, the Soviet Union, China, and the United States were at war with the Axis Powers of Germany, Italy, and Japan. By 1941, the scope of warfare was worldwide, with battlefronts in Europe, North Africa, the Pacific, East Asia, and nations from every populated continent involved in the global conflict. The Axis Powers had set their sights on global domination, with the plan of Germany overtaking continental Europe and the Atlantic, Italy commanding the Mediterranean Sea and surrounding countries, and Japan becoming the superpower of East Asia and the Pacific.

In the US, the Pearl Harbor attack by Japan's military "kamikaze" suicide-mission pilots led to unwarranted suspicion of people of Japanese ancestry. This is where the Japanese American community's tragic "incarceration" story began, as Executive Order 9066 was signed by President Franklin D. Roosevelt on February 29, 1942.

Executive Order 9066 commanded that all persons deemed a threat to national security living on the West Coast of the United States—including Japanese American citizens born in the US—leave their homes for "relocation centers" in remote desert wastelands. These nearly 120,000 Japanese American residents of Washington, Oregon, and California would have to leave behind their homes, schools, businesses, occupations, and farms for an unknown future.

No time was wasted in carrying out this government order, as the first internees were relocated to temporary detention centers starting March 24, 1942. This gave some less than one month to leave their homes, close up their businesses, sell their belongings and assets, and say goodbye to friends and neighbors.

The impact of Executive Order 9066 was devastating and unprecedented in American history. Many Japanese Issei, the first generation to immigrate to America, had lived in the US for twenty to forty years of their adult lives by this time. The Issei were business owners—farmers, gardeners, florists, restaurant owners, grocers, and more. Many of the Nisei were students or just entering college and careers. The majority, nearly 70%, were born in the United States, making them American-born citizens.

In 1940, 1,855 persons of Japanese descent, immigrants and US-born natives, lived in Orange County. The American-born citizens numbered 1,178 or 63.5% of that total.[18] Many children were school-age, born to immigrant parents who were mostly farmers. Seima had been in California for twenty-five years at this time, clearly a member of his community in Westminster and an established farmer.

History has proven that there were no espionage or disloyal activities among Japanese Americans or Japanese immigrants against America. The fear-driven action of this executive order was never warranted or justified. We cannot dismiss the racism that was apparent in this devastating action against 120,000 law-abiding citizens and legal residents.

To top it all off, at the time, no one knew how long this presidential order of incarceration would last.

The Munemitsus' future had become very uncertain.

. . . .

My parents always referred to these places of incarceration as internment camps, so I was quite shocked when I visited the Smithsonian Museum in Washington, DC, in 2017 to see the Smithsonian's display, "Righting a Wrong: Japanese Americans

18 John Needham, "War Spawned Vast Changes for O.C.'s Near, Long Terms," *Los Angeles Times*, November 11, 1991.

and World War II." The museum curators referred to the camps, not as internment or relocation camps, but as "concentration camps." This 1946 quotation from Harold Ickes, Secretary of the Interior, uncovered the true intent of the camps: "We gave the fancy name of 'relocation centers' to these dust bowls, but they were concentration camps nonetheless."[19] This change in terminology recognizes that the Japanese American residents and citizens sent to these places had been stripped of their promised freedom to work, have businesses, go to school, travel freely, and to participate in all other normal activities of everyday American life.

The Smithsonian noted government language that tried to soften the discrimination and racism present in the 1942 Presidential Order by using more palatable language. Now we understand that "exclusion" really meant eviction from their own property and livelihoods. "Evacuation" really meant forced removal; evacuations are for protecting one's life, not removing one from the only life one has ever known. "Internment" really meant incarceration. "Internee" really meant inmate. "Assembly centers," such as the racetrack stables that were used as the regional holding areas for the new inmates until the more permanent camps were built, really meant temporary detention centers. And "relocation center" really meant incarceration camp.

In addition, the display at the Smithsonian notes, "One of the most contested proposed changes in terminology is to designate the incarceration camps as concentration camps—a term still closely associated with Nazi death camps."

The meaning of words is important in history. As I refer to the forced relocation of Japanese Americans during World War II, I will use the term *incarceration*. The words *internment,*

19 The Smithsonian Museum, National Museum of American History, "Righting a Wrong: Japanese Americans and World War II," https://americanhistory.si.edu/righting-wrong-japanese-americans-and-world-war-ii.

incarceration, and *concentration* have been used to define this forced relocation. *The Merriam-Webster Dictionary* defines incarceration as "confinement in a jail or prison, the act of imprisoning someone or the state of being imprisoned." It also defines "intern" as a verb meaning "to confine or impound especially during a war."[20] Internment is the act of confining or impounding, with synonyms such as *captivity, confinement, impoundment, imprisonment,* and *incarceration. The Merriam-Webster Dictionary* defines "concentration camp" as "a place where large numbers of people (such as prisoners of war, political prisoners, refugees, or the members of an ethnic or religious minority) are detained or confined under armed guard—used especially in reference to camps created by the Nazis in World War II for the internment and persecution of Jews and other prisoners."

By definition, Japanese American internment camps were concentration camps. The Nazi death camps, however, were created with a different intention: that of killing a whole ethnic population. Out of respect for the more than six million Jews killed in the Nazi concentration "death camps" and millions more who suffered because of the Nazi regime, I will use the term *incarceration* in regards to Executive Order 9066.

Additionally, the term "internment" is the word assigned to the Department of Justice facilities, such as the one in Santa Fe, New Mexico, that were used to imprison men suspected of acting as spies for Japan. The designation of *internment* camp conforms to international law—per the Geneva Convention of 1929—for the treatment of prisoners of war. The War Relocation Authority (WRA) camps were operated under no such legal protections. The WRA, set up on March 18, 1942, was created to "take all people of Japanese descent into custody, surround them with troops, prevent them from buying land, and return them to their former

---

20 "Intern," *Merriam-Webster Online Dictionary.*

homes at the close of the war."[21] This means that the WRA camps are better understood as incarceration or concentration camps, rather than internment camps.

The truth is, we do not know what might have happened if the results of war had put America at greater risk and more on the defensive against Japan. Would all the Japanese American internees have been held as prisoners of war? There were barbed wire fences with military guard stations at these camps. The soldiers with loaded guns on watch 24/7 were not there for the protection of those inside. Rather, they were ready to shoot and kill any prisoners who tried to escape.

Those in the camps were left without answers—they only had their questions. When would the war end? *Would* the war end? What would be the outcome for these roughly 120,000 loyal Japanese American citizens and residents? What would happen to their homes, businesses, children? Would they lose everything they had worked so hard for? And would they lose their very lives?

Tad Munemitsu driving a tractor purchased with their hard-earned money.

21 War Relocation Authority, https://www.history.com/this-day-in-history/war-relocation-authority-is-established-in-united-states.

When Executive Order 9066 was signed, Seima and Tad had to make a tough decision: Should they sell their farm? At what price? And to whom? My dad, Tad, had just turned twenty, and now had to help make a decision that would affect his entire family and their future. Unfortunately, many saw this as a time to take advantage of the Japanese American's predicament, offering minimal amounts, paying pennies on the dollar for real estate, businesses, homes, farms and other assets owned by Japanese Americans. Should Seima and Tad take what they could or have faith that the war would end and they could return to Westminster to farm? This was not an easy question to answer when the whole world is at war, with no end in sight.

. . . .

In Japanese, the formal kanji characters for the word crisis, kiki, is 危機—the first character means danger and the second means opportunity. And that certainly fit the situation that Tad was in! Though the incarceration brought risk and potential for unknown danger for his family and future, could it also provide a hidden opportunity?

Tad knew that Mr. Monroe was a man he could trust. When Tad sought his counsel, Mr. Monroe thought of another option. Instead of selling the farm, what if they could lease it on an annual basis to another farmer? This would at least secure the ownership, and Mr. Monroe had faith that the war would eventually end. In those days, you either owned or rented space, but leasing a whole farm with equipment and all your household and farm belongings wasn't popular or widely practiced.

Given that every major world power was at war on both sides of the Atlantic and Pacific Oceans, it took bold courage and faith to believe the war would eventually end. Would anything, any country be standing at the end? How many would have to die before the fighting, the bombing, and the killing would cease?

With immense bravery and a hopeful attitude, the Munemitsus decided to lease their farm while incarcerated. This, however, brought about another pressing question: who would they lease a farm, farm houses, and farm equipment to in the midst of a war? Especially when many farmers were being "relocated" themselves? Who could be trusted with everything the Munemitsu family owned?

The answer didn't come immediately, but eventually Mr. Monroe remembered Gonzalo Mendez' dream of being a farm boss. Mr. Monroe made a call: "Gonzalo, you always wanted to be a farmer, perhaps this is your chance?" Gonzalo was interested, *very* interested! This was his chance to take his family back to a farming life as the boss of the farm, not the farm worker.

Kindness is...collaboration and
building trusted friendships.

With Mr. Monroe's introduction, Gonzalo and Felicitas drove out to the Poston incarceration camp to talk to Tad Munemitsu about leasing the farm. Tad and Gonzalo Mendez agreed on a one-year lease of the farm. The first lease document that I found was dated December 1944. It was followed by a second lease document, dated August 1945 through August 1946. The lease included the right to lease the forty-acre Munemitsu farm, including the family house, four small cottages for workers, the barn, tractors, trucks, and other farm equipment. It was a "move-in ready" farm. The asparagus crop was already planted, and, once planted, needed little care to harvest. It was the perfect crop to get started back to farming.

Though the lease with the Mendezes ensured that the farm would be cared for while our family was incarcerated, that didn't mean Seima and Tad did not suffer loss due to Executive Order 9066. As they'd built up their business, Seima and Tad had worked hard to buy farm equipment and tools. Sadly, in order to have money to take with them into the unknown future of the incarceration camp, Tad was forced to sell some of this hard-earned farm equipment to buyers who were only willing to pay prices far below market value. Many other Japanese Americans were also in this predicament of having to sell their hard-earned assets while buyers took advantage of them and only offered very low prices. But they had no other options. What would be provided in the camp? What would they need to live? Would they have opportunities to work and provide for the family? There were so many unknowns, and so taking some money with them seemed wise. The necessity of liquidating equipment and tools that he had spent much time and labor earning for such low prices was very bitter to my father, and there was a great deal of sadness in his voice when he talked about it.

No one knows if there might have been someone else overseeing the farm from May 1942 to 1944 or if there was another lease document that has since been lost. Another possibility is that there was an informal agreement prior to the first documented lease—and this seems likely, since Sylvia remembers celebrating her eighth birthday, in June 1944, on the Westminster farm, prior to the first lease document date.

Gonzalo was twenty-eight and Felicitas twenty-four when they moved their family to Westminster, where Gonzalo himself had spent much of his childhood. With big hopes and the chance

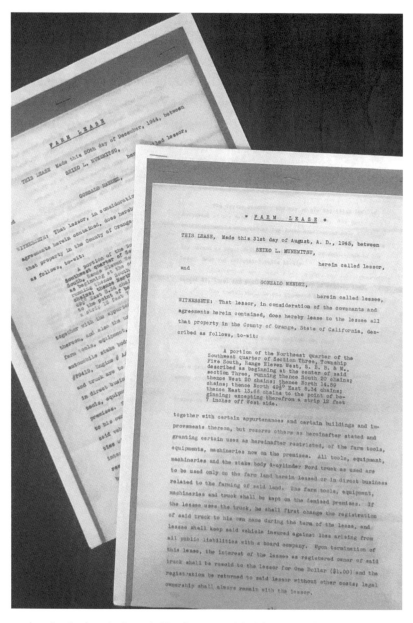

Leasing the farm to Gonzalo Mendez secured their home and future livelihood in the midst of an unknown future for the Munemitsu family. Two one-year farm leases signed between Seiko (Tad) and Gonzalo Mendez outlined the details of the agreement. The misspelling of Gonzalo's name on the first lease might be indicative of the rush to get the leases signed and official in a time of crisis.

for a dream fulfilled, they closed the Arizona Cantina in Santa Ana, gave up the lease for the restaurant, and moved on to the Munemitsu farm. The Mendezes rented out their house and the rental homes they owned, as this would ensure them a place to live in the future. Though he closed the Arizona Cantina, the lifelong friendships Gonzalo made in Santa Ana would endure into this next season of life. Gonzalo and Felicitas were excited to start a new adventure for their family on the Westminster farm.

CHAPTER 7

Faithful Citizens or Japanese Spies?

A few times in my life, I've been asked whether I or anyone in my family have ever been arrested. Under the assumption they mean arrested for an unlawful crime committed, I check the box indicating "NO." Though my family is far from perfect, we are Japanese by heritage and American by birth so doing anything like committing an unlawful crime would damage our "Family Name" (capitalization intentional). In Japanese culture, damaging the Family Name brings shame to the whole family, a lifelong sentence worse than death. But, truthfully, there needs to be a "YES, arrested, but unjustly accused" box for me to check.

While my father, grandmother, uncle, and aunts were forcefully removed and imprisoned as a part of Executive Order 9066, my grandfather, Seima, was arrested and held in a military prison facility and accused of being a spy for imperial Japan. On May 14, 1942, in Westminster, Seima was arrested by the FBI and taken to the Santa Fe, New Mexico, high-security Department of Justice internment camp. The only evidence against him was his involvement in the Kochi-ken Club, a social Japanese prefecture club, and his service as a board member of the Japanese language school for young children.

The Kochi-ken Club was formed by a group of Japanese Issei immigrants from Kochi Prefecture (a prefecture in Japan is equivalent to a state in the US). The members of the club wanted to preserve their old friendships and family connections, and also celebrate some of the cultural aspects of Kochi, their home state in Japan. They hosted New Year's Day lunches with authentic Japanese food and summer picnics with Japanese dance and games for their children. Many of the Issei formed these home-town clubs for immigrants. In fact, it would have been similar to many of the Italian and German immigrant clubs of that time. The club also met to share meals and stories, celebrate holidays with Japanese food and dance, and encourage each other in a foreign land. What Seima saw as staying socially connected to longtime friends from Japan and retaining for his family some innocent Japanese culture and language, was viewed by the US government as "spy" activity.

The Department of Justice (DOJ) internment camp was a military-run facility with twelve-foot-high barbed-wire fences and armed guards in towers, equipped with rifles and tear gas in the event of any escape attempts by the prisoners. Japanese men sent to Santa Fe were considered "dangerous enemy aliens," with the only evidence against them being their involvement in harmless Japanese community and religious organizations. At the DOJ internment camp, men awaited their cases being "tried," but their release required them to renounce their Japanese citizenship.

Knowing my grandfather, after being falsely accused of being a spy, arrested and taken from his home by the FBI, and having suffered the abrupt removal from his family without any assurance of when or if he would see them again, he would have found it difficult to know who he could really trust. As a legal resident of the US who was not a citizen, I'm sure he felt renouncing his citizenship from Japan was not a wise idea. Would he end up an immigrant without a country, arrested by the United States, now without any citizenship anywhere? If he were to renounce his Japanese citizenship, where would his citizenship lie?

Seima Munemitsu, top right, with other Japanese men unjustly arrested and held at the Dept. of Justice facility outside of Santa Fe, New Mexico.

He likely thought of keeping the option of returning to Japan with his family open, not in retaliation against America, but as a man responsible for his family. If he would not be allowed to stay in the United States, yet had also renounced his Japanese citizenship, where would he and his family go? What was to become of him? Who would provide for his family? Would he even see them again?

I also wonder how difficult the language barriers must have been for Grandpa and the other men who were primarily Issei and spoke mostly Japanese. How clear was the communication of these life-changing questions and decisions? After all, my dad, Tad, went with Seima to the bank to translate and explain business details. How much more important were the decisions he now was being forced to make separated from his son, translator, and business partner? Were there any trustworthy translators for them there at the DOJ camp?

From Santa Fe, Seima was sent to a facility for those who were higher security risks in Lordsburg, New Mexico, on June

12, 1942, about a month after his Westminster arrest. Lordsburg was run as a Prisoner of War (POW) camp and was the scene of the unprovoked shooting deaths of two elderly Issei captives on July 27, 1942. Toshio Kobata and Hiroto Isomura were shot and killed by a guard who claimed they were running toward a fence to escape. The guard was found not guilty, despite Kobata and Isomura's fellow inmates claiming that both men were physically weak due to previous injuries and could not run.[22]

Grandpa Seima would have been there at the time of the shooting and I'm sure it gave him and his fellow inmates even greater concern regarding the intention behind their imprisonment. Now, Seima was a POW in the United States, the country he had lived and farmed in peacefully for twenty-six years. The country that he called home. But now as a POW, his future was quite unclear. All Seima knew was that his family was being held in a desert incarceration camp in Poston, Arizona, about 480 miles away.

. . . .

Only a few short months after Executive Order 9066 was issued, the Munemitsu family, along with 120,000 other Japanese American immigrants and citizens, reported for transportation to the "internment" camps. While some families went directly to a remote desert incarceration camp, many Japanese Americans were put in temporary detention centers while the camps were being readied for internees. One such center was created at Santa Anita Park, which became Santa Anita Assembly Center, in Arcadia, California.

The government converted this horse-racing facility thirteen miles northeast of downtown Los Angeles into an "assembly

---

22 Lordsburg (Detention Facility), https://encyclopedia.densho.org/Homicide_in_camp/#Internment_Centers:_U.S._Army_and_Department_of_Justice.

center," and it operated from March to October 1942. It is estimated that anywhere from 8,500 to 18,000 Japanese Americans
were forced to live in the deplorable horse stables, while some
500 barracks were being built. But even with the barracks, only
a small percentage of the Japanese Americans there lived in
humane shelters. Most were doing the best they could to make
a horse stable a temporary home. Can you imagine being forced
from your home to a horse stable? I'm sure these families were
quite worried as they awaited orders, but perhaps very eager to
leave the wretched horse stalls, even if their next destination was
a remote desert incarceration camp.

Each Japanese American was allowed only one suitcase
to take with them to the incarceration camps. All household
belongings had to be sold or left with non-Japanese friends and
neighbors for safekeeping. The Munemitsu farm had a barn
where they, as best they could, locked up for safekeeping their
belongings that couldn't be carried. Some families left treasured
items in the garages and barns of trusted White friends, with
hopes that they would be allowed to return. And others just left
whatever goods they had with the homes they sold, not knowing
what the future held for them.

Both sides of my family lived in Orange County before the
incarceration: my father's family in Westminster and my mother's family in Santa Ana, though my parents would not meet
and marry until after World War II ended. My mother's father,
Makisaburo Sasaki, and his wife, Moto, farmed as much as 332
acres of sugar beets, chili peppers, and string beans. Makisaburo
and Moto had two daughters: my aunt Rakumi, just nineteen
years old, a graduate of Santa Ana High School and student at
Santa Ana College, and my mother, Yone, seventeen years old, a
junior in high school. The Sasakis lived on the outskirts of the city

of Santa Ana, and were established in the Santa Ana agricultural community, farming lima beans and sugar beets.

When Executive Order 9066 forced their relocation as Family #24202 to Poston, Arizona, they were blessed with kind neighbors who cared for their things with hopes they could return to Santa Ana. This was not just a suitcase or a few boxes. They left all their household belongings behind under their White neighbor's watchful care. I found this list in my aunt's 1942 handwritten diary, recording the boxes and trunks left with the Babylon family:

Stored at Bill Babylon's
Box 1 Sewing Machine
Box 2 Dishes, cups, bowls, plates, etc
Trunk 3 Trunk with Victrola and records
Box 4 Pots and pans, Trunk
Item 5 Washing Machine
Box 6 Books
Box 7 Pots and pans
Trunk 8 Trunk - Sheets and clothes
Box 9 Tools
Box 10 Tools
Box 11 Pots and Pans

*Kindness is...neighbors helping neighbors;
neighbors caring for their neighbor's
belongings as if they were their own.*

What would it be like to pack up everything you might need for an unknown period of time in one suitcase smaller than today's carry-on roller bags while being wrongfully imprisoned in the midst of a war? What would you take to live in the middle of a desert in a thin, plywood and tar-papered barrack where it was windy and cold or dusty and over one hundred degrees in the shade? This is the situation my grandparents and parents were in. Hardest of all, they had no idea when or if they would ever be allowed to return to their Orange County farms and homes.

As the government rolled out Executive Order 9066, the plan called for ten "internment" camps in all, each in its own desolate, unpopulated, and remote location, away from the more populated West Coast. Most of these camps were in high desert or plains climates, where the weather was bitterly cold in winter and scorchingly hot in the summer. The camp locations, each the size of a small city in the 1940s, became "home" during World War II to around 120,000 Japanese American residents called *internees*. Here are the locations and populations of the camps:

Topaz, Central Utah - 8,130
Colorado River (Poston), Arizona - 17,814
Gila River, Phoenix, Arizona - 13,348
Rohwer, Arkansas - 8,475
Jerome, Arkansas - 8,497
Manzanar, California - 10,046
Tule Lake, California - 18,789
Granada (Amache), Colorado - 7,318
Minidoka, Idaho - 9,397
Heart Mountain, Wyoming - 10,767[23]

Many of these incarceration camp populations were larger

23 Monument Photographs, https://www.njamemorial.org.

than most towns and cities in those areas. In fact, Poston's population of 17,814 people became the third largest "city" in all of Arizona. Not exactly something to be proud of, but it does show the impact of moving over seventeen thousand people from California into a desert along the Colorado River.

To add injustice upon injustice, Poston was actually put on the Colorado River Indian Reservation. The tribal council adamantly opposed the use of their land, as they did not want to be part of an injustice against the Japanese Americans. However, the tribal council was overruled by the War Relocation Authority, who took seventy-one thousand acres of tribal land to incarcerate the Japanese Americans.

Kindness is...speaking out for the oppressed and standing against injustice, even despite the injustice that you yourself have experienced and endured.

CHAPTER 8

A Family Separated and a Kindness Remembered

Now separated from Seima, my grandmother, Masako, and her sons, Tad and Saylo, were taken to the Arizona desert, just over the Colorado River to Poston, Arizona, to begin incarceration for an unknown period of time. They left on May 17, 1942, just three days after Seima was arrested. At that point, they must have wondered if they would ever see each other again. Would they be reunited as a family? And if so, when? Would they ever have their freedom back?

As the train left the Orange County station, another loss weighed heavily. My aunts, Aki (Akiko) and Kazi (Kazuko), were not with their mother, Masako, or their two brothers. Just seven years old at the time, the twin girls were suffering from chicken pox and ordered to stay in the local hospital, to avoid the spread of disease among those in the incarceration camps.

It is hard to fathom the turmoil Masako must have felt. First to have your husband accused and taken as a "spy," then to be ordered from your home, and now your young daughters aren't allowed to be with you. All this took place over the course of three dreadful days! These had to be the three worst days of my grandma's entire life! What agony she must have felt! Would she ever see her husband again? Would her daughters get well and be reunited with her? How long would it be?

Meanwhile, the twin girls were at the local hospital, feeling well enough to play but not fully healed from the chicken pox. They were so young that they didn't realize the severity of the crisis. They were totally unaware that the only childhood home they knew wouldn't be their home once they healed of the contagious childhood disease. Aki remembers not really understanding why they were separated from their mother, brothers, and their father. At the time, she thought that all children who got chicken pox went to the hospital and couldn't see their families until they get well. What a blessing that the twin daughters were sick together and had each other, and, at that young age, were naive about what was happening around them.

The nurses were kind to the girls and Popsicles were a daily treat. The nursing staff was compassionate, never letting fear trouble the young girls, and hiding the fact that the recovering girls were left in their care because their mother and brothers had been shipped to an unknown place and unknown future. After a few weeks—what must have felt like an eternity to their mother, Masako—Aki and Kazi were accompanied by a nurse, by train, to the Poston Camp. Going on the train was exciting and overshadowed any questions as to why they were going so far by train, and why by train at all, when they had originally been driven by car to the nearby hospital.

Not only did the nurses at the hospital make sure the girls were healthy, but they also cared for their emotional well-being by not telling them they weren't going back to the home they knew, or that their mother was hundreds of miles away in a desert camp. Thanks to the kindness of these nurses, Aki and Kazi didn't have to suffer terror while they were separated from their family.

A mix of cultures: Masako with twin daughters, Kazi and Aki, in Japanese kimonos with American baby dolls. This would have been taken before the forced evacuation to the Poston, Arizona, incarceration camp.

Kindness is...keeping children safe and well,
even children of another mother.

Aki recalls not realizing that something was wrong until she saw her mother, Masako, waiting at the train platform with tears rolling down her cheeks. Tears of love? Tears of joy? Tears of relief? Likely all of these emotions flooded in as she was finally reunited with her girls. Reunited but not returned to the home she longed for. And though Masako was together again with all her children, she still was yet to be reunited with the husband she loved, Seima.

The two young girls wondered where their father, *Pops* as they lovingly called him, was. Why was he not there at the train station to greet them as well? And when would they get to see him again?

Amidst the injustice and the tragedy of having to leave her home without her husband and twin daughters, Masako experienced kindness from others who knew discrimination. She would always say, "Be very nice to Black and Mexican people." Of course, she meant that we must be nice to all people, but especially Blacks and Mexicans in a culture where they were regularly and persistently mistreated. This simple phrase was deeply rooted in Masako's heart. When speaking about her experience, Masako always said how kind and nice the Black and Mexican train station employees and porters had been to her, a young woman accompanied only by her two sons, as they left for the Poston Camp. They were exceptionally kind to her in her darkest days and she never forgot their kindness.

Since Masako didn't speak English well, and was amongst a mass of Japanese Americans trying to board a train, I wonder exactly how my grandma experienced their kindness and how it must have made her feel. I ponder what that must have been like, to receive kindness from unfamiliar men of color doing a job. This was in contrast to others who were unkind: some White neighbors who now jeered at her Japanese face, and perhaps the FBI agents who took Seima away. Were there others who perpetrated similar unkindness? Others who showed no compassion toward a terrified and hurting young mother?

The term *omoiyari* is a Japanese word meaning to have sympathy and compassion towards another person. I'm not sure there is a direct translation of this word in English, but it includes being kind and considerate, having compassion, feeling empathy, and so on. Translations of this word explain that this quality of omoiyari is considered universally necessary for a society to be sustainable. Perhaps what makes omoiyari different from other forms of sympathy is that it typically is shown in an action or a response, not just in a feeling, toward another person.

Masako's life, safety, and any sense of security she had crumbled in a blink. It is no wonder the kindness of the Black and Mexican men that worked at the train station meant so much to her. I suspect they knew the pain of racism, prejudice, and discrimination. Their genuine gestures of kindness came from a deeper place than mere customer service. Those train station employees had omoiyari to my grandmother, and she never forgot that.

No, this injustice was not directly against their families or those who looked like them, but they had no doubt that what was happening to her could happen to them. Maybe not this time, but on another day and in some other unjust situation, it could be them. To echo my friend Joe's words, "It wasn't just *us*."

Kindness is...omoiyari: sympathy and compassion shown and demonstrated for others.

CHAPTER 9

Trading City Living for Life on the Farm

Open farmland in Orange County is very rare today, so it might be hard to imagine that most of Orange County was rural farmland at the start of World War II, and Santa Ana was one of the few cities. Moving from the city of Santa Ana, with lots of neighbors on tree-lined streets and paved roads, to a forty-acre Westminster farm, was a big change for the Mendez family, especially for Sylvia and her brothers. But it was a change that they thoroughly embraced.

Throughout their lives, the three siblings have often talked about the memories they made while living on the farm, and every story starts out proudly with "when we lived on the farm..." The rest of the family has heard this so often that the younger Mendez siblings make up stories and say confidently, "When we lived on the farm too," even though they weren't yet born at the time the family resided there.

Certainly the forty-acre Munemitsu farm had all the makings of one big playground for the three adventurous Mendez children. The farm had a big house where the Munemitsu family had lived, and which the Mendez family would now call home. In Santa Ana, the Mendezes had indoor plumbing, bathtubs, and toilets. The farm had none of these luxuries. Yet living on the farm was such an adventure that the Mendez kids didn't mind giving up the indoor conveniences they were used to. Sylvia loved the big wooden ofuro (Japanese-style) bathtubs, which seemed more like fun pools to a child. All three Mendez children could take a bath in them at the same time. She also recalls big white pot urinals in each bedroom. Without an indoor toilet, these pots would help the family with any late-night restroom emergencies. Sylvia also remembers the undesirable chore she and her brothers shared of taking the urinals out in the morning.

Sylvia had her eighth birthday (June 7, 1944) on the farm in Westminster. She and her brothers made so many memories while they lived on the Munemitsu farm. They could run and play all over the fields. There were so many places to play hide-and-seek. They would play marbles in the dirt, and toy soldiers with other children who lived nearby and came to play on the farm. There was an owl in the barn that made it fun and kind of spooky. And there were domesticated animals too! Tad had left Jackie on the farm, an old brown workhorse that the kids played with. Sylvia's mom, Felicitas, bought three pigs—a white one, a red-brown one, and a black one. And they had chickens running all over the farm that provided eggs for the family.

The Munemitsu family farm house, Westminster, where the Mendez family lived.

Sylvia remembers how sandy the soil was at the Munemitsu farm. It was perfect for digging, and she and her brothers dug a big hole in the sand near the workers' cottages and the bath-houses. This was the perfect place for the shallow hole. It was near the irrigation ditch so that water could easily be diverted to fill the six-foot-wide "swimming pool." It was so shallow that they actually could only sit in it, but the children felt great pride that they built it themselves. They would play and sit in it for hours on hot summer days.

This barn was on the Munemitsu farm in Westminster. Sylvia, Gonzalo Jr., and Jerome spent time playing in and around this barn as children on the farm.

Together, Gonzalo and Felicitas ran the farm, both driving the tractors and taking care of the fields. Gonzalo did the book-keeping at night. They drove the tractor to harvest the asparagus as the braceros followed after the tractor, collecting the harvest to be packed at the farm's packing house. The harvest was then transported by truck to the Alameda Wholesale Produce Market in Los Angeles.

There were fourteen braceros who worked on the farm and lived in the four cottages on the property. Now, Felicitas cooked for the braceros, as well as her own family, just as Masako Munemitsu did before Executive Order 9066 removed them from Westminster. Now Felicitas was cooking in the same big kitchen where Masako once cooked. And it was here that Sylvia first learned to make tortillas and chili sauce when she was about nine years old.

The asparagus crop was harvested and crated at the big packing house on the farm. Felicitas went back to the Santa Ana barrio to recruit friends and family as workers to come pack the asparagus in crates for delivery to the wholesale market in Los Angeles. From the wholesale market, supermarket buyers would buy the produce to be shipped to grocery stores all over the western United States.

In addition to the Munemitsu farm, Gonzalo and Felicitas leased a twenty-acre farm nearby from Mr. Blue. Here they grew tomatoes that were packed up in the packing house and sold to the wholesale market. Sylvia fondly recalls eating the big, red tomatoes, fresh from the field, and her mother scolding her and her brothers for eating too many and spoiling their appetites for dinner!

When the Mendezes moved to Westminster, they had lots of money saved from their cantina business. Gonzalo felt that with their savings and the money they would be able to make on the two farms they leased, they would be able to buy their own farm one day. This exciting dream helped the Mendez family settle in on the Munemitsus' Westminster farm well, and it looked like it would be a great place to raise their family. That is, until September rolled around...and it was time to enroll for school.

CHAPTER 10

Life Behind Barbed-Wire Fences

While the Mendez family settled into their new home, the Munemitsu family—minus Seima—tried to adapt to their unfamiliar situation in Poston, Arizona. Masako, Tad, and Saylo were now Family #24132, assigned to Poston Camp 1, Block 44, Barrack 6B. Akiko and Kazuko, once cleared of the chicken pox, arrived later than the rest of the family and were given a separate number from their mother; they were designated #20344 A and #20344 B. This perhaps made them the youngest internees with a family number different than their mother's.

Poston consisted of three designated sections known as Camp 1, Camp 2, and Camp 3. Each camp was made up of many structures. For instance, Camp 1 had twenty-seven blocks of barracks, a school, a hospital, and an administration area. Camp 1 was the largest of the three camps, with almost nine thousand people living within its boundary—about half the population of the entire incarceration camp. It was a mile square in size, with thirty-six blocks. A camp "block" consisted of fourteen barracks, a mess hall, a communal men's latrine with open shower room, a women's latrine with open shower room, a laundry/ironing facility, and a community hall.

Barracks were twenty feet wide and a hundred feet long, and housed four families each. The barracks were constructed of redwood and pinewood, covered with tar paper but without any other insulation in the walls. Poston was unique in that the barracks did have double roofs to try to offset the 120-degree heat in the desert summers.[24] Each family had a twenty-foot-by-twenty-five-foot area for their living quarters. There were no sturdy walls between each family unit, just a flimsy, thin wall or curtain. The family "apartment" was usually just enough space for beds, and maybe some chairs and a table.

For those used to their own very modest Japanese culture, these living conditions—the crude family sleeping quarters, the lack of privacy, the shared bath and outhouse-style toilet facilities, just to name a few—caused much shame on top of the shame they already felt being sent to the incarceration camps. They were used to being very private, and placed a high priority on cleanliness and sanitation. This whole situation upended not just comfort, but their whole identity as a culture. The Japanese women did the best they could with the food in the mess hall; it was certainly not the fresh fish or produce of Japanese cuisine that the mothers were used to making.

Masako, Saylo, and Tad reunited with Kazi and Aki in Poston, Arizona, after the girls recovered from chicken pox and were brought separately to the camp.

24 Information taken from the program passed out at the Poston Camp 1 fifty-year reunion (1992), page 8.

To add further insult to injury, the camp administration at Poston sent out a letter to the internees stating it was up to the residents to make Poston a "model" community. After removing them from their homes, businesses, schools, and communities, now they were told to make this barren desert of shantytown barracks a model community? A mimeographed May 28, 1942, letter to all residents of Poston from the Poston project director reads:

> Poston has been set aside as a relocation center, and what it develops into is entirely dependent upon the colonists themselves. If each and every person in the community will assume his full share of the responsibility and do his full share of work, Poston can be made into one of the model communities of the country. To accomplish this end, and to create a community of which every member can be proud, it is vital that everyone make his full contribution.

"Colonists" *choose* to settle in a location; what Japanese Americans were facing was a forced removal. Yet, the War Relocation Authority administrators of the camps expected the Japanese Americans to "make their full contribution." Despite this insensitive and audacious request, with a spirit of fortitude and self-preservation, the Japanese Americans at Poston did in fact fight to make the most out of the unspeakable injustice they faced. They set out to create a unique community and life with shantytown resources. The adults found work to do within the camp, serving each other and each other's families with the few resources they had. They built buildings for schools out of adobe bricks, and organized children's activities and cultural clubs. They tried to envision what else they could do to make this desert camp livable for an unknown future.

Both Aki and Kazi, only seven years old at the time, started going to school inside the camp behind the barbed-wire fence. Aki remembers walking to school along a dry streambed on a hot and dusty desert path and across a narrow bridge that spanned a desert gully to school. The school building was a long adobe-brick building, quickly constructed by the incarcerated internees.

Aki and Kazi were in the third and fourth grade at the Camp 1 school. There were about twenty students in the class, and Aki fondly remembers that her teacher, Miss Smith, was a wonderful teacher who really cared for the students, despite the difficult situation. She had moved in order to take this job to educate the Japanese American students in Poston. Though there were some White teachers among the internees, Miss Smith was not one of them. Aki recalls never thinking of Miss Smith as a Black woman until after leaving the camp. What were the circumstances that led Miss Smith to become the only Black teacher to teach at Poston Camp 1? It's impossible to know, but now, as an adult, Aki wonders what the rest of Miss Smith's story was.

In the Poston camp, the Japanese American children were given school lessons authored by the Federal War Relocation Authority. While the academic subjects, like reading and mathematics, were pretty typical of what they were used to back home in Westminster, there was a new, noticeable focus on loyalty and nationalism. These American-born citizens would pledge their allegiance to the United States every day in the camp school. Imagine, as a child, after being forced from your home and school, saying those words at the same time you were unjustly incarcerated, without the liberty or justice the pledge promised. How confusing it must have been to pledge allegiance to the very country whose government had taken away the only freedom you knew!

Despite all this, the resilient young children of the Poston Camp also found their silver lining. After school, Aki and Kazi found ways to "play" in camp. Aki remembers that while her mother, Masako, worked in the camp's kitchen to feed people hundreds of daily meals, she and Kazi would play kitchen in their own way. It was so hot in the summers that they heard people say, "You could fry an egg on the sidewalk." As two industrious little girls, they thought they would try! Sneaking eggs from the kitchen, they found a very hot spot on the sidewalk, cracked the eggs, and waited intently for them to sizzle. Disappointed that they only had an eggy mess on the sidewalk, they retreated to the shade to cool off! Those eggs might not have fried, but these two young girls felt like they were continually baking in the sizzling hot desert sun.

Average summer temperatures could be as hot as 110 degrees Fahrenheit and average winters could be as cold as 40 degrees Fahrenheit. And those were the averages, so in a given year, temperatures might range from 10 degrees in winter to summer highs of over 125 degrees! And that was just the temperature; the wind also presented many unpleasant issues.

"Dust. And more dust. And wind. Dust and Wind." This is how Poston was often described to me by my family. The winds would blow either burning hot or frigid cold. The wood barracks had holes and cracks all over where the desert sand and dust would blow in. Sweeping it up was a constant activity. All the women in the Munemitsu family are "expert broom sweepers"; the title is an acknowledgment of the daily chore of sweeping the desert sand out of their barrack rooms in Poston.

Though the Arizona desert didn't have the noticeable green vegetation of California's more temperate regions, it did get lots of sun. The industrious and curious farmers and gardeners decided to see if they could grow vegetables and create desert gardens, irrigated by streams siphoned from the Colorado River, which was about three miles away. Gardeners even created a Japanese-style garden that included a bridge, gazebo, and small pond. Some vegetables, like the leafy greens of lettuce and spinach, grow very fast in the desert when well watered and cared for. What might not grow in coastal California in winter, did quite well in the sunny desert winter. In fact, the land where the camp once was is still agricultural today. Poston locals still credit their agriculture industry to these seemingly random farming trials that were created by the gardeners and farmers interned at Poston.

Amidst this harsh climate, the Japanese American internees fought hard to build a semblance of community in the camp. While it was hardly "model" in typical American terms, they worked, organized, and built a small town of services, complete with a post office, police and fire crews, hospital, church, camp administration, and block management structure. Internees built and worked in a dry goods store, legal aid center, elementary and high schools, sewing and bird-carving schools. They even built a tofu factory to bring some Japanese food to the internees.

There were Japanese American doctors, lawyers, pastors, teachers, and others who all went to work providing services that the community of eighteen thousand needed to meet their everyday needs. Before the camp, the families had worked hard to support themselves. The bare barrack housing with cots and basic foods were provided by the government, but everything else needed to make this home in the desert was created, built, or bought by the internees.

A general store co-operative was established as a community enterprise to provide a place to shop for other groceries, confections, fabric to sew clothing and curtains, and toiletry needs. Shoe repair shops, hair salons, and barbershops were also set up by the internees to serve the community. Churches were established for Sunday services in the Buddhist, Catholic, and Protestant traditions. Sports teams were organized for weekend free time, with all the equipment being purchased by the camp teams themselves. The internees established all the essentials of everyday life within the camp, all without their normal incomes and without the businesses they had been forced to leave behind.

SCHOOL OF TAILORING - CLASS 1945
POSTON, ARIZONA. K. URATA, Principal

The Japanese Americans tried to create a community of learning skills and working in Poston. One example is this 1945 picture of the students of the School of Tailoring, organized by the Japanese Americans to teach tailoring skills. Note the school auditorium on the far right, built by the Japanese Americans to provide educational and sports facilities for the schoolchildren and the community.

To keep the camps running, the government paid wages for the essential workers and their services in food preparation, construction, education, and health care. Novice and unskilled workers received twelve dollars per month, skilled workers received sixteen dollars per month, and professional or highly educated internees, like doctors and lawyers, received nineteen dollars per month. This was hardly enough to pay for the essentials a whole family needed, and the internees had to depend heavily on their own savings to purchase necessities. Women needed fabric and thread to sew curtains for the bare barrack windows. Small desks and bureaus were made out of scrap lumber purchased by the internees to furnish the living quarters. Small lamps and chairs were needed to furnish their living spaces. And during the very hot summers, ice cream and sodas were welcome treats that could be purchased at the co-op store.

The staff of the camp Employment and Leave Office, Block 27, Camp 1, Poston, Arizona. My mother, Yone Sasaki, worked there in the camp and is pictured in the front row, center.

A camp newsletter called the *Poston Chronicle* shared news and activities for the camp of eighteen thousand. They organized Boy and Girl Scout troops for the children. For cultural entertainment, they built a theater stage for music and dance performances and community social gatherings. There was much to do to try to bring some sense of "normal" daily life to the camp, because they didn't know how long the war would last. While they made the best out of the situation, they still yearned for the "liberty and justice for all" that was noticeably absent behind these barbed-wire fences.

Meanwhile, Masako received letters from Seima. These letters were censored for details, but at least she knew something about his captivity and that he was alive. In her efforts to reduce fear and anxiety for Aki and Kazi, she told them that "because the government thinks your father is important, he is being held in a separate camp, so do not worry." Masako held her emotions deep down to normalize the situation for her daughters. For their emotional welfare, she never made a big deal out of all they were facing. Aki and Kazi assumed their father's situation was similar to Poston, but in a different location. Little did they realize Seima was a POW, tried and judged dangerous enough to be held under strict military guard in New Mexico.

. . . .

One thousand eight hundred sixty-two people died, about 11% of the total number of internees, from medical problems in the camps.[25] Most certainly they weren't given the health care available in their city hospitals, and the harsh climate certainly contributed to a decline of health for the ailing. It is estimated about 10% of the deaths were from tuberculosis, which is highly contagious, especially in crowded communities like the one housed in Poston's weathered barracks.

Among the many who perished in the desert camp was my maternal grandmother, Moto Sasaki. Ailing, Moto went to see the Poston camp doctor in July 1942, soon after arriving in Poston. She spent many weeks in and out of the camp hospital, but just

---

25 Medical Care in Camp / Hospitals at Full Capacity, https://encyclopedia.densho.org/Medical%20care%20in%20camp.

eight months after entering the Poston camp in May 1942, Moto died at age fifty-two on January 4, 1943. I've read a sad account of her hospitalization and of daily family visits to the Poston camp hospital in my aunt Rakumi's diary. My aunt said she likely died of stomach cancer, but Moto's death certificate listed congestive heart failure and hypertension, which makes me wonder if she would have survived had she been in a Los Angeles hospital.

Rakumi and Yone were now left without the home they knew and without the mother they dearly loved. The loss of their mother was "the worst day of my life," as Rakumi wrote in her diary. This surely overshadowed the miserable living conditions of the camp and left them numb, feeling abandoned in their grief and loss. This trauma would plague their sense of security for the rest of their lives, and left them feeling abandoned, cut off from the maternal love they adored.

Focusing on what she could, my mom, Yone, wrote a letter to Santa Ana High School, asking for assurance of her graduation diploma for completing the senior year schoolwork she'd taken with her to camp. The letter she received back was reassuring and compassionate regarding her plight. The school assured her that she would receive her diploma on completion of the self-study materials she took with her, and asked her to say hello to and advise the other Santa Ana High School seniors that their diplomas would be granted as well. The letter genuinely expressed how sorry the school administrators were that the students couldn't be with them and how they were sorely missed. My mom must have gotten great encouragement from the letter, as it is a keepsake she saved for the rest of her life. Despite being forced to miss the cap and gown procession of graduation while in camp, she was proud to be a Santa Ana High *Saint*, Class of 1943.

*Kindness is...words of compassion and
encouragement when facing an unknown future.*

CHAPTER 11

Separate Is Not Equal:
Going to School in Westminster

The Mendez family settled into living on the Westminster farm throughout the summer of 1944. But all good things have to come to an end, and, in this case, the end was a beginning: the start of the school year in September, when the Mendez children went to be enrolled in a local school.

Over the summer, Gonzalo Mendez' sister, Soledad Mendez Vidaurri, her husband, Frank, and their children moved to Westminster from Northern California to help on the farm. They were experienced farmers and the two families wanted their children to grow up together. In 1943, Soledad, known as Aunt Sally to Sylvia and her siblings, took her two daughters, Alice and Virginia, and the three Mendez children to enroll them at the Seventeenth Street School, as it was the school closest to the farm. This was the elementary school that the Munemitsu twin girls, Akiko and Kazuko, went to before they were removed from their farm home, so it was logical to enroll the children now living on the farm there. The cousins all got ready that day and headed off, brown paper lunch bags in hand, eager to start school together.

When they arrived at the school office, the woman at the office counter looked at the children and told Aunt Sally that her fair-skinned daughters, Alice and Virginia, could be enrolled at Seventeenth Street School if she would say they were of Belgian descent! Belgian? That was ridiculous! Then Aunt Sally was told that the Mendez children would have to enroll at the Hoover School. How absurd! Why could the Vidaurri girls go to Seventeenth Street School, but the Mendez children could not? They were all Mexican after all!

Though Sylvia does not remember why the Vidaurri daughters would have been allowed to attend Seventeenth Street School, it was likely because her cousins were more fair-skinned and their last name didn't sound Mexican. Fuming with anger, Aunt Sally refused to enroll her children at Seventeenth Street. The Vidaurris would not have their children attend unless the Mendez children could also. Aunt Sally, with the five children following her, left the school, unsure of what would happen next and, more importantly, of where they would go to school.

The next day, Gonzalo and Felicitas went to Seventeenth Street School to try to resolve the issue. But they made no progress with the Seventeenth Street School administration. Gonzalo elevated the issue to the school district superintendent. But the superintendent was no help and insisted the Mendez children go to Hoover School. Gonzalo and Felicitas didn't stop there, however. They eventually went to the Orange County school board, but their request was turned down again there. This continuing injustice left the Mendez and Vidaurri parents rightfully angry and extremely frustrated.

Hoover School was not at all like Seventeenth Street School. For starters, it was next to a cow pasture that had an electric fence that bordered the school yard. It was legal for a livestock yard to have an electric fence with a live current, but a school? This fence gave any unknowing young student a dreadful shock if they accidentally touched it or played too close to it. There was no protection for the young school children from this hazard.

Furthermore, the curriculum at Hoover assumed that the children couldn't speak proper English and didn't have the intellect to learn subjects like math and science. In fact, teachers at Hoover only taught very basic conversational English, under the assumption that the children were not English speakers yet. The truth was, though, that Mendez children already spoke English well. Students who spoke any Spanish at school were reprimanded and told to only speak English.

Sylvia also recalls the teachers teaching the girls embroidery and cooking. She felt like they were training them to be maids and house cleaners, and providing them no real academic focus. Sylvia, Gonzalo Jr., and Jerome were so disappointed and upset about the poor quality of education that the Hoover School offered. This was not like the school they had attended in Santa Ana, where they were used to subjects like reading, writing, math, history, and science. Remember, prior to their move to Westminster, they had attended Fremont School in Santa Ana, and while Fremont was for all the Mexican students in the barrio neighborhood, the curriculum and subjects were no different than Franklin School, where the White students went.

Seventeenth Street School had high-quality teachers teaching typical school subjects like reading, writing, math, history, and science. The Mendez children knew the academics at Seventeenth Street School were similar to their school in Santa Ana, because their friends who came to the farm to play with them attended Seventeenth Street School. As a young girl, Sylvia remembers longing to go to school with the friends she played with on the farm. She also longed to enjoy the safe playground at Seventeenth Street School during recess and lunch breaks. She did not want to go to a school that had a fence with an electrical current, offered poor educational content, and didn't even have a playground for recess.

Even getting to Hoover School was demeaning for the Mendez and Vidaurri children. The school bus would pick them up on Edwards Street, at the dirt road that led to the farm. On the bus, they were with all their friends, the White children in the neighborhood that surrounded the farm. The school bus would drop all the other kids off at Seventeenth Street School, but Sylvia and her brothers couldn't go in. They would say goodbye to their friends and then have to walk to Hoover. It was almost a half mile further away physically, but emotionally, the distance felt even longer and more humiliating. It was just another reminder of how some wanted to distance themselves and their children from Mexicans. It was a constant reminder of the discrimination and prejudice of the school and school district administrators.

They were all equal enough to take the same school bus, but not equal enough to go to the same school.

Sylvia, Gonzalo Jr., Jerome, Alice, and Virginia did go to Hoover for a short while. However, since they were not learning much at all, they frequently chose to read and study books at home. Going to Hoover was a waste of time for them. They needed and wanted academic subjects, not training to be cooks, seamstresses, and house cleaners.

Gonzalo didn't want his children to go to Hoover School at all. He remembered facing this same issue as a boy. He, though, was able to attend Seventeenth Street School because they allowed him an exception. He and his friends had proven their scholastic ability and need for an education that was more challenging.

But now it was clear that, in all those years, things had not changed for the better. Perhaps things were even worse now for his children. Unless he did something about it, Hoover was the only school option for his children while living at the Westminster farm. Unless he did something about it, this discrimination would persist for all Mexican children.

Gonzalo decided he would not rest until he could do something—not just for his children, but for all children. He desperately wanted to right this wrong that was now affecting another generation of his family. In talking to his friends and business colleagues in Santa Ana, he learned that other families were in the same situation in other school districts in Orange County. As he talked to other people about this discrimination affecting his children, Gonzalo heard similar stories of school segregation in Orange County school districts. This was not just his family's problem. It was a problem throughout Orange County and the entire state of California. In California, school districts could enforce different discrimination rules against any non-White children at their own discretion.

Some Mexican families were willing to talk to Gonzalo, while others felt there could be negative repercussions and chose to not go public. However, none of these families had legal experience, and certainly they had no expertise in taking a case to court. It would take a lot of help to elevate this inequity to justice. Who would be willing to help them? And how would they pay for this legal aid?

Gonzalo had made a new friend since he started farming in Westminster: a man named Henry Rivera. Henry was a truck driver who delivered produce to the Alameda Wholesale Produce Market. Henry came by the farm daily to pick up the asparagus in order to transport it to market in Los Angeles. He would also bring food scraps from restaurants in Los Angeles for Felicitas to feed to her pigs. Henry would bring big bags of leftover white lima beans to Felicitas, who would cook them in a big pot before feeding them to the pigs.

When Henry heard their story of local school discrimination, he told them about an attorney in Los Angeles, Mr. David Marcus, who had recently won an anti-segregation case in favor of Mexicans in San Bernardino, California. This case involved

Mexican Americans being denied the right to use the public swimming pool. Gonzalo was encouraged and he contacted Mr. Marcus to see if he would take on their children's case.

Kindness is...caring enough to help a friend find a solution to his problem.

Attorney David Marcus (1904-1982) was of Jewish descent, born as an American citizen in Iowa. His parents had immigrated from Tblisi, Soviet Georgia, around the turn of the twentieth century. His father founded stores in Albuquerque and Los Angeles, and David attended elementary school in Des Moines, Iowa, and high school in Albuquerque, New Mexico. He attended the University of California, Los Angeles and earned his law degree at the University of Southern California in 1927.

David Marcus had firsthand experience of discrimination and injustice. As a teenager, he played the violin and was excited to participate in a recital. He was permitted to perform, but had to play behind a curtain as the recital organizers would not allow a Jewish performer to be seen. Imagine his humiliation. The young man was clearly good enough to perform, but due to anti-Semitism, he was not allowed on the stage with the other performers or to be seen by the audience.[26]

Mr. Marcus had been married twice; his second wife, Maria, was the daughter of a physician and an immigrant from Mexico. He and Maria raised their daughters to be bilingual in English

26 Strum, *Mendez v. Westminster*, pg. 39-40.

and Spanish. Marcus had his own law practice, specializing in immigration and criminal law. One of his clients was the Mexican Consulate. He spoke Spanish well and often travelled to Mexico for his clients. David Marcus became known as the "Mexican Lawyer" for his work on behalf of Mexicans—even though he himself was Jewish.

Meeting Mr. Marcus was a divine appointment for Gonzalo. Mr. Marcus told Gonzalo that California law permitted the segregation of some children (Indians/Native Americans and Asians), but that this law did not include Mexican Americans. Together, Gonzalo and his new attorney began to canvas other Mexican American families in Orange County to ask about their experience with Mexican schools. The more people they talked to, the more they found that this was a widespread problem, and they were successful in gathering the much-needed evidence.

Marcus and Mendez rallied four other families in Orange County to stand against school discrimination with them. These families also had children who were not permitted to go to the White schools in their districts, despite all speaking English well. Because lack of English language proficiency was the main justification the school districts gave for segregating the Mexican Americans, the children's language skills were an important point supporting the Mendez case. Furthermore, no English language tests were given to evaluate the students' language skills. How then were these school districts deter mining a student's English level? It was clear that language deficiency was being used as an excuse for prejudice.

In addition to Gonzalo and his children—Sylvia, Gonzalo Jr., and Jerome—the additional plaintiffs were four families: William Guzman and his son Billy in the Santa Ana School District; Frank Palomino and his children Arthur and Sally in the Garden Grove School District; Thomas Estrada and his children Clara, Roberto,

Francisco, Sylvia, Daniel, and Evelina in the Westminster School District; and Lorenzo Ramirez and his sons Ignacio, Silverio, and Jose in the El Modena School District. By being a part of a class action lawsuit, these families were speaking up on behalf of about five thousand other persons of Mexican descent: the citizens and residents of the four school districts of Westminster, Santa Ana, Garden Grove, and El Modena.[27] Together, these families became the core of the class action lawsuit known as *Mendez, et al. v. Westminster School District of Orange County et al.*[28]

The next issue was paying Mr. Marcus and funding the lawsuit. Fortunately for Gonzalo, vegetable prices were high during the war years, as so many Japanese American farmers were incarcerated in the camps. The asparagus and tomato crops brought in a healthy income and Gonzalo decided to take $500 (which would be approximately $7,100 in 2020) of his hard-earned farm profits to retain Mr. Marcus on the case. This would be only the first payment of many by Gonzalo toward the legal costs of this case. The fact that Gonzalo was both the one who contracted with Mr. Marcus and the one who served as the major funding source of the case is the main reason why "Mendez" was the first name listed in the case title of *Mendez, et al. v. Westminster*. In addition to the money put up by Gonzalo, volunteers went door-to-door in the local Mexican American communities, collecting donations one dollar at a time to help fund the case. It might not have added up to a lot of dollars, but it did raise awareness and support among the community members and made all the Mexican Americans feel like they were united in this cause. Gonzalo retained Mr. Marcus and they began meeting weekly to strategize how to fight and win the case.

27 Strum, *Mendez v. Westminster*, pg. 61-62.

28 *Et al.* comes from the Latin phrase meaning "and others" and typically stands in for two or more names (source: *Merriam Webster Dictionary* online). Here it is used in reference to the other families and the other school districts that were part of the case.

*Kindness is...using what you have
to further what you believe.*

While Gonzalo did the grassroots organizing—retaining the attorney, convening the families, setting up legal-strategy meetings—Felicitas ran the farm. She cooked meals for the braceros, planted the tomato crop, took care of the farm animals, and harvested the asparagus and tomatoes—all while raising her three children on the farm. Sylvia recalls that her father was "always in meetings" during this time and her mother was very busy with the household and farm.

In addition to overseeing the farm, Felicitas organized a community effort for moral support while Gonzalo and Mr. Marcus began gathering evidence for the case. She contacted other parents and together with them organized the *Asociación de Padres de Niños Mexico-Americanos* (Parents Association of Mexican American Children), which showed the school districts that the Mexican American community was behind this case.[29] Certainly this was a sacrifice of time, talent, and treasure for the Mendez family. A sacrifice that generations of California students would benefit from in the future.

---

29 Strum, *Mendez v. Westminster*, 42.

*Kindness is...sacrificing for the good of those you
do not know, even the generations to come.*

As the case took shape and was filed, the negative publicity was heating up for the Westminster School District and other school districts in Orange County. The administration at the Westminster School District did not want this case to go to court, and offered Gonzalo a compromise which actually was a bribe. If Gonzalo "would stop this nonsense," then the school district would allow the Mendez children to go to the White Seventeenth Street School. But this was not enough for Gonzalo. He was firm in his commitment to fight this case for all the children of California, not just the children of his family.

At this time, Sylvia recalls that her father worked hard on the case. As a young child, however, she didn't fully perceive what this was all about. "I never realized back then that my parents were fighting for equality, freedom, and justice...I just thought they wanted us to be able to go to a beautiful school with a nice playground...not the horrible school with the electric fence!"

CHAPTER 12

Silent Voices, Silent Protest

While the Mendez family was fighting for justice in Westminster, over one hundred twenty thousand Japanese Americans were in the middle of a fight of their own. US school history textbooks didn't include the Japanese American incarceration for nearly forty years after World War II; in some places even as many as fifty years passed before it was included. Even today, many people have never heard of this sad and horrible part of US history. I recently met someone in their forties who lived and grew up in the southeastern part of the US before moving to California in 2019. Though educated and holding a doctoral degree, he had never heard of the Japanese American incarceration until he went to a nearby California historical site that mentioned it. When hearing about it, many ask, "Why did the Japanese Americans not protest and resist being herded into the incarceration camps? Why did they put up with this injustice?"

While my family and the majority of Japanese Americans did not outwardly protest, there were protests. Most notable is the case of *Korematsu v. United States* in 1944. Fred Korematsu was a US citizen born in Oakland, California (1919–2005). His Issei parents had immigrated from Japan and ran a floral nursery business. Fred was a Nisei, and never doubted that he was an American citizen. He tried to enlist in the US Coast Guard and National Guard when the US entered WWII, but was denied because of his Japanese ancestry. He was also the victim of discrimination when fired from his job as a welder because of increasing prejudice against Japanese Americans.[30]

As Fred's family readied to go to the incarceration camps under Executive Order 9066, Fred, in his early twenties, resisted, changed his name, and claimed to be of Spanish and Hawaiian descent, partly in an effort to stay with his White girlfriend in Oakland. He was discovered, arrested on May 30, 1942, and sent to the county jail in San Francisco. The ACLU (American Civil Liberties Union) contacted Fred to see if he was willing to be a test case in challenging the constitutionality of the internment order. Fred accepted the ACLU's proposal, but was eventually convicted in federal court for violating the order. He was placed on five years probation. From jail, he was sent to Tanforan Assembly Center and later to the Topaz, Utah, incarceration camp where the rest of his family was interned.

This did not deter Fred. He and the ACLU appealed the case all the way to the US Supreme Court. Sadly, Fred's case was defeated again on December 18, 1944. The court, out of loyalty to the president and military, ruled that the mass incarceration of West Coast Japanese Americans was warranted out of "military necessity." The court falsely justified their decision, citing the perceived likelihood that Japanese Americans were communicating with the enemy, imperial Japan, and therefore prone to disloyalty. However there was no evidence—and never has been any evidence—of Japanese American disloyalty or involvement with Japan's attack on America.

In June 1983, the Commission on Wartime Relocation and Internment of Civilians (CWRIC) concluded that the "internment" of Japanese Americans and Japanese immigrants was motivated

---

30 "Fred's Story," The Fred T. Korematsu Institute, https://korematsuinstitute.org/freds-story/.

by "race prejudice, war hysteria, and a failure of political leadership." Decades later, in November 1983, Judge Marilyn Patel of the US District Court, San Francisco, overturned Korematsu's conviction, finally righting a wrong after nearly forty years. Fred spent much of the rest of his life as an activist for civil liberties.

In 1998, Fred received the nation's highest civilian honor, the Presidential Medal of Freedom, from President Bill Clinton. In Fred's own words to Judge Marilyn Hall Patel, US District Court, San Francisco, 1983:

According to the Supreme Court decision regarding my case, being an American citizen was not enough. They say you have to look like one, otherwise they say you can't tell a difference between a loyal and a disloyal American. I thought that this decision was wrong and I still feel that way. As long as my record stands in federal court, any American citizen can be held in prison or concentration camps without a trial or a hearing. That is, if they look like the enemy of our country. Therefore, I would like to see the government admit that they were wrong and do something about it so this will never happen again to any American citizen of any race, creed or color.[31]

Ironically, on the same day a divided Supreme Court ruled 6-3 on the Korematsu case—stating that the detention of West Coast Japanese Americans was a "military necessity" not based on race, upholding the government's action to incarcerate one hundred twenty thousand innocent men and women during World War II—the same court unanimously declared this incarceration unjust when hearing a lesser-known case fighting for

31 Quotes by Fred Korematsu, https://korematsuin-stitute.org/freds-story/, and https://charactermedia. com/5-quotes-by-fred-korematsu-that-remind-us-to-say-never-again/.

Japanese American freedom. This battle was fought by Mitsuye Endo. This young woman and her legal team were successful in proving the injustice of incarcerating loyal Japanese Americans during World War II.

Mitsuye, a native of Sacramento, California, was a young woman working a clerical job at the California Department of Employment when Pearl Harbor was bombed. In the aftermath and fear, she was dismissed from her job because of her Japanese ancestry. Interned with her family at the Tule Lake, California, camp, she was contacted by the Japanese American Citizens League's (JACL) attorney to challenge the incarceration of loyal Japanese American citizens in the courts. She reluctantly agreed, as she didn't want to bring attention to herself. However, in her words, she did it "knowing it's for the good of everybody."

Mitsuye was selected because she was seen as the ideal plaintiff: an American citizen who had never been to Japan, who didn't speak Japanese at all, a Protestant with a brother who had served in the Army. The petition was filed on July 13, 1942, in the San Francisco federal district court. Subsequently, she was moved to the Topaz, Utah, camp while her suit went through the court system. Though she was offered the opportunity to leave the camp early (an offer the government made with the hope of negating her court case), she opted to remain in camp as leaving would nullify the lawsuit. A year and a half went by as the case slowly progressed to the US Supreme Court. Her case, *Ex parte Mitsuye Endo*, was finally ruled in her favor on December 18, 1944, a unanimous court decision. This meant that the government could not detain or incarcerate citizens who were loyal to the United States.[32]

32 Korematsu v. U.S., https://encyclopedia.densho.org/Korematsu%20v.%20 United%20States; and Mitsuye Endo, https://encyclopedia.densho.org/Ex%20 parte%20Mitsuye%20Endo%20(1944). Also, Stephanie Buck, "Overlooked No More: Mitsuye Endo, a Name Linked to Justice for Japanese-Americans," *The New York Times*, Nov 15, 2019.

*Kindness is...sacrificing your freedom to fight
for the freedom of the whole community.*

The contradictory rulings of these two Supreme Court cases announced on the same day are confusing and appear to be some type of political compromise to justify the actions of the president's Executive Order. Despite the 1983 overturning of Korematsu's conviction by the US District Court, the 1944 US Supreme Court ruling against Fred Korematsu still stands.[33]

. . . .

As to why others did not more actively resist, the answer to this question is complex, so the context is important. The Pearl Harbor attack in 1941 was the first major attack on US soil by a foreign power since the first world war. This attack brought a great sense of unexpected fear to all Americans. America was at war, and the question loomed, *When and where might we be attacked again?* Since imperial Japan was the perpetrator of this attack, Japanese Americans were looked at with suspicion and unjustly accused of being spies. Some Chinese Americans even put up signs in their homes and stores that read, "We are NOT JAPS!"

Fueled by fear, the US government was looking now at these hardworking Japanese American citizens as traitors and as a threat to the communities in which they lived. Some Americans threatened their Japanese neighbors with words and weapons. Fear and shock ruled their days. When their own government

---

33 https://korematsuinstitute.org/freds-story/.

turned against them, making them out to be the "enemy among us," the one hundred twenty thousand Japanese Americans who were to be incarcerated didn't stand much of a chance.

In this volatile environment of fear and anger, most of the Japanese American community chose to do what was ordered. They were accused of being disloyal citizens of the United States, so they would prove their loyalty by dutifully sacrificing their freedom and self-respect. They would do what was seen as peace-keeping for the sake of the whole society. In an unconventional way, this was their form of resistance. To show they were not disloyal, they would go on trying to be the best possible citizens they could.

There were many Japanese American men who served in World War II. The Nisei Japanese American men of the US Army's 442nd infantry regiment signed up to fight in Europe and their courage gave them the distinction of being the most decorated unit of its size and length of service in US military history. By April 1943, a total of about fourteen thousand Nisei men served overall in the 442nd, earning more than eighteen thousand awards in less than two years. This included over four thousand Purple Hearts, four thousand Bronze Stars, and five hundred sixty Silver Stars, twen-ty-one Medals of Honor, and seven Presidential Unit Citations.[34] Their motto, "Go For Broke," and their nickname, "Purple Heart Battalion," testify to the courage and loyalty they displayed, despite the fact that their Japanese American families and friends were being held in incarceration camps as "the enemy" without freedom.

Those who didn't serve in the military during the incar-ceration also thought it important to prove themselves to be trustworthy, industrious Americans. So, both during and after the war, they worked toward lifelong careers, applied for college

---

34 "Go For Broke Part Two: The 442nd Regimental Combat Team," September 24, 2020, https://www.nationalww2museum.org/war/articles/442nd-regimental-combat-team.

in the Midwest and East Coast, became doctors, judges, lawyers, accountants, architects, and other highly educated professionals as valued and capable members of their communities. Others worked hard to be farmers, gardeners, grocers, and small business people of integrity, serving their towns and cities. Again, most of all, they wanted to prove themselves loyal and hardworking citizens.

Another layer that is important to understand has to do with the values and worldview of traditional Japanese culture. It is very characteristic of this culture to repress emotions, holding true feelings of anger, resentment, and despair deep within. Surely there was a wide range of emotion never expressed publicly nor healed internally. Being obedient to authority is also of high value in traditional Japanese culture. This was undoubtedly at play during these tumultuous times.

Furthermore, as an Asian "shame-based" culture, accusations that Japanese American citizens and long-term residents might be traitors in the US severely wounded the sense of loyalty these families felt. This triggered deep feelings of shame in the hearts of the Japanese, regardless of whether that shame was warranted. The attack on Pearl Harbor was extremely shameful because the enemy was imperial Japan and the kamikaze bombers were of Japanese descent.

In a shame-based culture, the people bear the burden for the whole community, and in this case, the innocent Japanese Americans bore the weight of this shame. Probably in some ways, they felt they had to do what was being asked of them, because they knew they were immigrants and a minority culture. Even the US-born citizens among them likely had some feeling of being in a foreign land because of the color of their skin, shape of their eyes, and their Japanese last names. Not to mention the clear confirmation of shame that came from being falsely accused, forced away from their homes and communities, and incarcerated without constitutional American freedoms.

Two other innately cultural characteristics of the Japanese people are what is known as *gaman* and *gambatte*. Gaman is a Japanese Zen Buddhist term that means "enduring the seemingly unbearable with patience and dignity." This characteristic of gaman obviously influenced the response of Japanese Americans to the injustice they faced. Gambatte is a phrase that even I remember from my childhood. It can mean *good luck, do your best*, or *you can do it*. When spoken as I remember, the inflection is stoic—it implies persevering through anything. You *can* do it, you *can* make it, *never* give up. This is the underlying intention.

This never-give-up spirit helped the Japanese American community persevere in the midst of extreme hardship. Sadly it also came with an emotional price tag. Bearing the weight of this shame through self-fortitude alone led families who survived the incarceration to carry great anxiety, pressure of perfectionism, and underlying fear that this unfair incarceration could happen again. The Japanese Americans in the incarceration camps knew and lived gaman and gambatte. The shame of being accused and the trauma of being in the camps never left, and the many emotional wounds inflicted by this experience were never fully healed.

After the war, some Japanese American families never spoke of their incarceration history to their children, the next generation. It was a hidden secret within the family. Post-war American history books never mentioned this part of history either. Many wanted to pretend as if it had never happened. I can't even imagine the shock of the children whose families chose not to speak of the "camp" incarceration. How would you begin to ask your parents about a significant part of their lives left untold? Why was camp never mentioned?

I'm sure talking of these awful memories brought back many hurts, trauma, and emotional pain for most. This gave the families that chose not to speak of it good personal reasoning to not discuss it. And I am sure the families who chose to speak of it to their children had good reasons also. In our Munemitsu family, my parents chose to discuss this period of time in their lives. It was referred to as "camp days," and they told me stories about the dusty and difficult living they experienced behind barbed wire fences, in small shared living quarters, suffering the loss of their freedom.

These hardships were balanced by all the friends my parents made as young adults living in the desert, as well as the memorable work and activities they did to pass the time. Conversations with their "camp days" friends included who met who, when and where, where they lived before the war, who were the camp "rebels," how hot and dusty the summers were, as well as how cold and miserable the winters were. They were all young adults in camp, so the magnitude of the loss and shame was endured by this community of new friends together. They found the strength to accept their reality and make the best of it with the support of the community.

I don't recall these conversations being angry, bitter, or emotionally charged at our house, as the years of freedom and hard work to reestablish themselves in their communities had healed some old wounds. I remember the time together being more focused on the sharing of the long three-year experience that now was partially redeemed by lifelong friendships. Our family had its own way of putting the past in the past and moving on.

My parents and their "camp family" friends identified each other by which camp they were sent to. Family stories are also casually categorized as "before camp" and "after camp," designating the situation and context of the memory. I remember my parents would identify friends by saying, "they went to Manzanar," or "they were in Poston with us," as if they were alumni of a school or members of a club in their young adulthood. The camp you were sent to also identified where you lived before the war, but it was the camp location identification that was first in their minds. "Camp days" was a real part of our family history, shared by other friends in the Japanese American community. It became part of all our histories and to some degree, that generation's identity. It is their Nisei badge of survival.

Kindness is...a community sharing
difficult life experiences together.

Growing up, I thought all Japanese American kids knew about the incarceration camps, even though my White friends did not. But I never even questioned why it wasn't in the history books. This provides an important example for us all: just because something isn't recorded in a textbook, that doesn't mean it didn't happen. It is vital that *all* of history, the truth good or bad, be told and shared. We can learn from both the human victories and the injustices of the past, such as racism and false judgments.

Though being forced to live in a desolate desert incarceration camp didn't make the headlines at the time—nor the history books after WWII—many Japanese Americans continued to dream of a better life. Many of the young Japanese American adults had dreams of being first-generation college students and hopes for a career of their choice. Would the camp incarceration prove to be a dead end, or merely an obstacle to be overcome?

CHAPTER 13

"Indefinite Leave" Status Opportunities

One opportunity that the young Nisei adults took advantage of was "indefinite leave" from the camps. With this opportunity, Japanese Americans could apply to leave the "internment" camp they were incarcerated in for a time, to work or attend school. Indefinite leave approvals were granted mostly to young adults and college students. The catch was, they could not return to the West Coast. Obviously, possessing only a suitcase and little in the way of money, a person pursuing indefinite leave also had to have a college scholarship or a sponsoring family to live with.

Tad Munemitsu was granted indefinite leave from Poston in October 1943 to go to Denver, Colorado. There he worked first for United Produce, harvesting crops, and then for American Brake Shoe & Casting, in the foundry. Tad went from the furnace-like heat of the Arizona desert to work near real furnaces that melted metals into castings for military and industrial use. He also found work doing very physical labor on the road construction crews in Welby, Colorado. Before the war, my dad had attended Fullerton Community College in California to study business, but now he took whatever work he could get.

Meanwhile, Seima had been returned to the Santa Fe DOJ prison, leaving behind the Lordsburg higher-security-risk POW facility in November 1942. Another year and half passed, and Seima was finally "paroled" in November of 1943 to Welby,

Colorado, where he was reunited with his son Tad. This ended his time in the Santa Fe, New Mexico, Department of Justice internment camp. But the move to Colorado was not freedom. Within twenty-four hours of his arrival in Colorado, he had to report to a parole officer in the Denver office of the Immigration and Naturalization Service and would continue to do so every week while there. Now he was "a paroled POW" but at least he was with Tad. The two of them would often work together while both in Colorado.

After ten months in Colorado, Seima left Colorado and was reunited with Masako, and daughters Aki and Kazi, at the Poston, Arizona, incarceration camp on August 18, 1944. They were all still in an incarceration camp, but Seima and Masako were together. I cannot imagine the relief my grandparents must have felt once they were reunited. The kids of course were excited too. "Pops" was back! This was nearly two-and-a-quarter years, or twenty-eight months, after Seima had been taken from his wife and family back on the farm in Westminster.

This, however, did not bring the whole family back together. Tad was in Colorado and his brother, Saylo, was in Iowa, both on indefinite leave. Saylo recalls his father telling them, "Don't do anything to shame the family, this country, or yourself." This reflected the values of an Asian shame-based culture. Saylo told his mother when he left Poston that he wanted to go to college and become a doctor, knowing this would make her happy.

He first worked at a factory, making camouflage netting for the war effort, and then applied to a number of colleges. Unfortunately, he was rejected by the colleges he applied to because he was Japanese American. Finally, through a friend, he heard that Carlton College in Northfield, Minnesota, was accepting Japanese American students. He applied and was accepted! Saylo worked on campus in many different jobs. After graduation, he went on to the University of Iowa Medical School, where he eventually graduated as a surgeon. Like many Nisei, going to college during "indefinite leave" meant Saylo didn't have to return to the incarceration camps and could remain at college in Iowa for the rest of WWII and, after that, for medical school.

My mother, Yone, and aunt Rakumi were also granted "indefinite leave" to go east from the dry, hot desert to Cleveland, Ohio. Rakumi had started her studies at Santa Ana Community College, but had to leave to enter the Poston incarceration camp in 1942. After about eighteen months, Rakumi left the Poston camp to go study at Fenn College, living with the Coppedges of Shaker Heights in Cleveland, her sponsoring family. In the Coppedge home, she became what she called a "Girl Friday," which meant she was a general household helper. It was out of the kindness of the Coppedges' hearts that they took Rakumi in as a young college student, and that became the start of a lifelong friendship.

Kindness is...friendship and care from strangers in faraway cities.

This education greatly benefitted Rakumi in her career in bookkeeping and accounting. Though she never completed a formal degree, Rakumi worked for various accountants and for Munemitsu Farms as their bookkeeper and general office administrator from 1952 through the rest of her working life. On May 13, 2011, Rakumi was awarded an honorary associates degree from Santa Ana College posthumously. I accepted it on my aunt's behalf. This was part of the California Nisei College Diploma Project, a result of California AB37, which required the California public college system to retroactively grant honorary degrees to any student of Japanese American descent, living or deceased, who was forcibly removed and incarcerated during World War II. I know Auntie Rakumi, at only four foot ten, would have loved to have donned the cap and gown that day, but sadly this happened five years after she passed into heaven.

My aunt Rakumi Sasaki (center) in Cleveland, Ohio,
with her welcoming host family, Mrs. Coppedge
(right) and another family member, in 1943.

In March 1945, after almost three years at Poston, my mother, Yone Sasaki, followed her sister to Cleveland and worked at Ferro Enamel Corporation until World War II ended. Her time in Cleveland was short, as the war ended in 1945, but she made some sweet friends in her work department. I wonder how it must have felt for my mom and aunt to receive kindness and friendship from virtual strangers in Cleveland. After being forced from their home and farm in Santa Ana, what a heartwarming gift to know others were willing to give them a chance to go to school and work—to be essentially rescued from the camp life they were subjected to as young adults. They both made new friendships in Cleveland, some of which continued throughout their entire lives.

Kindness is...strangers becoming new friends for life.

Rakumi Sasaki (left) with friends after leaving the dry and dusty Poston, Arizona, incarceration camp barrack homes for winter in snowy Cleveland, Ohio.

My uncle, Aki's husband, Dave Nakauchi, was a young teenager during the war. His family was granted "indefinite leave" and left camp to go to New Jersey to work at Seabrook Farms, then the largest US producer of canned vegetables. To meet the growth of the company in the 1940s, Seabrook began to hire Japanese American families from the camps to work in the cannery in 1944. The living and housing conditions there were not much different than the incarceration camps. Yet the Japanese American adults were eager to leave the desert to go to work, even for long hours at low wages. They were still living behind chain-link fences without full freedom, but it felt more normal and productive working there than living in the isolated desert camps.

Dave went to school at Seabrook with other Japanese American and White children whose parents all worked at the cannery. It was at Seabrook that Dave recalls his first encounter with racial profiling. One boy questioned if he was Japanese and Dave answered in perfect English, "Yes, I'm Japanese American."

"But *you* look like *us*. You don't look like a monkey," the boy stated honestly, after looking at Dave's back end to check for a tail. "The Japanese we see in the newspaper all look like monkeys!" The boy was referring to satirical drawings of Japanese people with buck teeth, Coke-bottle thick glasses, and tails like monkeys. "You're not a monkey!"

No, my uncle Dave is not a monkey, though he has a great sense of humor and is always eager to have fun. He is not a monkey, and Japanese Americans are not monkeys—despite what the 1940s wartime news media and political "comics" portrayed.

The media wanted to portray people of Japanese descent as less than human, and used their influence and voice as a divisive tool. Instead of truth and facts, the media encouraged division and increased prejudice in the country. This naive White schoolboy, who had never seen a Japanese American before, actually believed the media he saw and thought that the Japanese had tails like monkeys. How important it is to see all people, regardless of race, country of origin, nationality, or tribe, as human, not lesser beings or caricatures of animals. How right the young schoolboy was when he met my uncle Dave: "*You* look like *us*."

Kindness is...treating every human as human, understanding that everyone is "like us."

CHAPTER 14

Freedom to Go Home: the War Ends

While Gonzalo and the other families continued to meet with Mr. Marcus, the deadly World War II raged on. The war had taken a horrific toll in the form of human lives lost. Families and friends mourned their loved ones. It is estimated that, in total, over seventy to eighty-five million were killed worldwide, whether in battle as military, or as innocent civilians killed by bombings, starvation, disease, and genocide.

This includes the Holocaust, where six million Jewish people were killed by the order of Adolf Hitler, the leader of Nazi Germany, in his attempt to eradicate an entire race of people. The millions of Jews killed made up nearly two-thirds of Europe's Jewish population. The worldwide death toll for World War II is unimaginable, as every survivor lost someone and some, overseas, lost the majority of their families, neighbors, and community. No one living, not one, was spared the loss of a loved one's life.

Even as Mr. Marcus worked with Gonzalo to fight against injustice and school segregation in California, he likely had no idea of the persecution and genocide that his Jewish brothers and sisters—people with the same ancestry as him across Germany and greater Europe—were facing at the time. Only decades later would the truth of the Nazi death and concentration camps be fully known. This is another case of a tragic untold history being fully and truthfully uncovered decades later.

A deadly closure to the war finally came, as the United States detonated two nuclear bombs in 1945. The first was aimed at the city of Hiroshima, Japan, on August 6, and three days later, on August 9, the second was aimed at Nagasaki, Japan. Both cities were major ports of naval, military, shipbuilding, and industrial significance for Japan. Japan surrendered to the Allies on August 15, 1945, but only after what is estimated to be up to 226,000 lives were lost in the bombings of Hiroshima and Nagasaki. Those killed were mostly civilians—fathers working, mothers caring for families, school children, neighbors and friends living the life typical of 1940s Japan. World War II officially ended on September 2, 1945, with the formal signing of the surrender by Japan's emperor to the United States.

Months earlier, on December 18, 1944, Mitsuye Endo's victorious Supreme Court case was announced the day after President Roosevelt gave orders that the Japanese Americans could begin to leave the camps and return home starting January 1, 1945. In reality, it took nearly all of 1945 for the internees to leave the camps. Endo's willingness to fight—and courage to not drop her case in exchange for her freedom—had effectively brought pressure through the Supreme Court decision to end the Japanese American incarceration in camps. Finally, there was hope that the Japanese American families could return home.

The whole world had changed, but for the Japanese American families in the incarceration camps, this meant freedom. They could go home. But most of the Japanese American families had been displaced for well over three years in the remote incarceration camps, and now that they were allowed to leave, the next decision loomed: *Where do we go?* If they still had homes or farms, it was easy to decide to return. However, many had sold everything before going into the camps, making it difficult to know if "home" was really "home" anymore.

To make matters worse, each internee was given $25.00 ($356.91 in 2020) to travel by train back home, and to reestablish themselves. They were expected to find a place to live and start a new life. Freedom at last, but how were they to start fresh with a mere $25.00? Even ten times that in 1945 would hardly be enough to rent a place to live, provide food, household goods, furniture, and transportation. How were they expected to start life over again?

Though they now had freedom to leave the camps, the new challenge to reestablish their lives began. Many Japanese Americans did not know what the future held. Some went where they had friends to stay with as they got reestablished. Others who had taken "indefinite leave" chose to stay in the midwestern and eastern areas where they had jobs or were now enrolled in college. This became a diaspora, a migration and scattering, of the Japanese Americans living in places other than the homes they had left on the West Coast. Some families decided to restart their lives in places like Idaho, Colorado, Illinois, and other parts of the Midwest and eastern United States.

Amid the celebrations of the war ending, groups of compassionate Americans remembered the Japanese Americans and reached out to them in ways they hoped would be helpful. My aunt Rakumi told of outreach efforts in Cleveland inviting the Japanese Americans on "indefinite leave status" living in Cleveland to stay and make Cleveland their postwar home.

A brochure, "How Can We Help Japanese American Evacuees? Suggestions for Church Women," written by Gracia Booth in November 1944, was published by the Committee on Resettlement of Japanese Americans, and sponsored by several faith-based organizations. The suggestions included offering employment and assistance in finding housing, organizing "meet the train" welcome groups, inviting former internees to do things together, and inviting them to organizational meetings. It also suggested that real and lasting friendships could come from inviting the Japanese Americans to your home and taking the time to visit theirs in return. I don't know how many of this brochure's readers took action, but I believe some did follow through and that their actions made a difference. It must have made a healing impact on my aunt Rakumi as she kept this brochure until her death over sixty years later.

Kindness is...caring for those who have been discriminated against and looking for ways to welcome them into the community.

My mother's family, the Sasakis, were one of the few fortunate enough to have a home to return to. I remember my mother, Yone, and my aunt Rakumi talking about their return to their Santa Ana farm home after the war ended. Since both had received approval for "indefinite leave," they were living in Cleveland, Ohio, at the end of the war. Instead of just returning to the next state over, they had to make a cross-country trek. They had a Japanese American family friend from Orange County who was now in Chicago on his "indefinite leave." He had worked, gotten married, and now he and his wife had a baby boy. He had earned enough to buy a car during his "indefinite leave." My mom and aunt took a train from Cleveland to Chicago and then drove back to the West Coast together with their friends.

This was the first road trip ever for my mom, and I know it marked new life and freedom for her as a young woman. She told me of riding in the back seat of the car, windows rolled down, and taking turns holding the baby boy, all the way from Chicago to Santa Ana. With the meager wages she had saved, she bought postcards of the American West to remember the places and sites they journeyed past. She kept these postcards all these years and I still treasure them today. They are a reminder of the new freedom and redemption of the hardships they endured. Their gambatte spirit had finally redeemed the years of incarceration at the Poston camp and they were again free to live as citizens of the United States of America.

My father's family, the Munemitsus, also had a home to go back to. Though it was still under lease to the Mendez family, the Munemitsu family had an address and surviving possessions. It had been almost three and a half years away from their Westminster home and farm. Three and a half years without their freedom had passed. With Poston closed by the fall of 1945 (the last incarceration camp closed in March 1946), the Munemitsus were at last heading home.

CHAPTER 15

Two Families on the Farm

I can only imagine the emotions my grandparents must have felt to be able to leave Poston and return to the Westminster farm. Tad's work in Colorado had given him the chance to save and buy a car to drive to Arizona and pick up the rest of his family. How wonderful it was to have the family together again! With Tad at the steering wheel, Seima, Masako, Aki, and Kazi rode by car over the Colorado River, the state line of California, through the Mojave desert to Orange County. I'm sure they smiled, laughed and cried tears of joy as they drove through the desert, eager to get home. And as they got closer to Westminster, they passed familiar businesses, schools, and other Orange County landmarks that brought back wonderful memories of life "before camp."

When the Munemitsu family left their Poston address of *Block 44 - Barrack 6 - Unit B*, they were blessed to have an address to go home to—13603 South Edwards Street, Westminster, California. This was the address of the farm that was now, in 1945, shared by two families: the Mendez family and the Munemitsu family.

Just the month before, in August 1945, the farm lease that Tad had signed with Gonzalo Mendez was up for renewal or termination. Hopeful that the war was coming to an end, Tad and Gonzalo agreed to a most curious arrangement for the next year-long lease, one that secured both families a place to live and work for another year. The lease included that the buildings on the ranch were to be used as dwellings by the lessor [Tad Munemitsu] for the "dwelling of his family or any person he designates" without cost or charge of rent. Also, the lessee [Gonzalo Mendez] agreed to "furnish the lessor and his family with such work as is available on and around the farm herein leased and to pay the minimum of prevailing wages to each person so employed."[35]

In an odd, but practical, arrangement, the owners of the farm became the employees of their farm's renter! My grandfather and dad, Seima and Tad, began to work for Gonzalo at the minimum prevailing wage. Tad Munemitsu's IRS tax form shows his employer as Gonzalo Mendez in 1945. This arrangement worked well and lasted for almost a year, from September 1945 to the end of August 1946. Gonzalo's dream of being the boss of a farm had been realized, with the owners of the farm his unlikely farmhands! It was a "trading places" situation. At the end of the lease, Gonzalo would take the profit from the asparagus harvest to pursue his plan to own another cantina.

Kindness is...working together,
regardless of who owns what.

Grateful that Gonzalo and Felicitas had been loyal and trustworthy caretakers and honest farmers during their absence, my grandfather and dad could begin to see a better future ahead. In a conversation I had with Sylvia, she told me the gratitude was

---

35 Mendez Munemitsu Farm Lease August 1945; Munemitsu Family Collection, Chapman University Library Archives.

mutual between the families. As a little girl, Gonzalo and Felicitas told her how they were grateful that they were not kicked off the farm when the Munemitsu family returned from camp.

"When your dad and the family came back, we worked and lived together on the farm," recalled Sylvia. "My father, Gonzalo, had no money to move since he was spending it on paying the attorney fees and getting the case to court. But your dad, Tad, worked it out with my dad. My dad would take the profit from the next crop of asparagus to start up another business. Tad was so nice, working together with my mom and dad to make sure they got a good fresh start too."

I think my dad, Tad, was just so grateful to Gonzalo and Felicitas, and grateful that the lease had worked out well for both families. Gonzalo got a chance to farm. My dad and the family had a home and farm to return to after the war. And as history would have it, the asparagus crop profits from Gonzalo and Felicitas' hard work paid the initial cost to fund the legal case that fought for all the children of the state of California, regardless of color, to go to desegregated California public schools.

Kindness is...collaborating together
for a win-win solution.

Gonzalo and Felicitas continued to live in the main house with their three children. My grandparents, dad, and two young aunts moved into one of the four workers' cottages on the property. It didn't really matter where they lived on the farm. They were home! Seima and Tad invited some family friends who had nowhere to go to come live in the other workers' cottages on the property until they could get back on their feet. Meanwhile, my uncle Saylo stayed in the Midwest to finish college and his medical school training, before relocating to California in the 1950s.

Some ask if there was ever any question that the farm was well cared for during the years of the lease to the Mendez family. After all, my dad leased the farm and literally everything they owned—the house, the barn, the farm equipment, the land—to someone he had just met. So, did the Mendezes care for the Munemitsu property well? The answer was unquestionably, *yes*!

Remember Gonzalo Mendez was recommended by his trusted banker, Mr. Monroe. The word of a trusted friend is of immense value, and Mr. Monroe was certainly a trusted friend. At that time, Tad could trust Mr. Monroe more than he could trust the rights of citizenship promised by the United States Constitution. This meant many of the normal questions of integrity were answered prior to the lease. The Mendez family could be trusted because Mr. Monroe trusted and knew them. What a difference a trusted friend and the integrity of others make in times of uncertainty and the unknown, when it looks like your whole world is falling apart!

> *"A friend is always loyal, and a brother*
> *is born to help in time of need."*
> —*Proverbs 17:17, NLT*

In addition, Gonzalo had made an extra effort during the war, displaying his integrity. Early in the lease period, Gonzalo was concerned that the lease money would not actually reach Tad. Several times, he drove from Westminster, nearly two hundred and fifty miles one way, across the California desert and Colorado

River, to deliver the lease money to Tad at the Poston Camp. This was a long drive, probably at least five to six hours one way through the desolate California desert—without the interstate freeway and air-conditioned cars that exist today. With today's wide Interstate 10, gas stations, rest stops along the way, and high-speed cars with air conditioning, it is still about a four-hour drive one way. No doubt this was a sacrifice for Gonzalo for the benefit of our family in Poston, but he did it to care for our family in camp.

Kindness is...sacrificing your time and effort for the sake of others.

Sylvia recalls how fun it was, as a young child, to have new playmates on the farm! She now had girls to play with, not just her brothers. She remembers Aki and Kazi, new girlfriends to play with outside and in the big kitchen. At bath time, Sylvia could talk to them from her side of the wall in the big Japanese ofuro bathtub, while Aki and Kazi would be in the adjacent bathhouse in their own ofuro bathtub. For young children, it felt like a spa retreat since no suburban house had three-foot-high bathtubs in adjoining rooms! Not only that, but these bathtubs had wood-burning fires under them to heat the water...a true childhood novelty!

Aki remembers that Sylvia was a very smart and mature young girl. They would run around the farm, play in the old barn, and make up games together. Meanwhile, she remembers

Gonzalo Jr. and Jerome being very "rough and tumble" boys, climbing up and jumping down from high places in the barn, which elicited stern warnings from their dad, Gonzalo.

Sylvia also learned a few Japanese words then, but the only one she remembers is "benjo" or bathroom, as in "I have to go to the bathroom." Other Japanese American kids came to visit and play at the Munemitsu farm. Sylvia distinctly remembers all the Mexican and Japanese American kids playing together. She especially remembers a cute young boy named Jun that she had a nine-year-old's "crush" on.

Such was the carefree life of children on the farm, despite the inequality that existed at the school district and state levels. Neighbors were friendly and all the children played together, and accepted each other as close friends. By doing this they overruled school officials' mandate that Mexican children should be segregated from their White playmates.

Kindness is...loving friends of all colors.

I love hearing what a young Sylvia and my aunt Aki remember about that time. What stands out most to me is that, even in the midst of significant racism and discrimination, the children flourished as equals. They had not been taught to see each other as different, without worth, or less-than because of the color of their skin or shape of their eyes. They just saw each other as people, as human, as friends.

My aunt Aki remembers her father and brother Tad working with Gonzalo on the farm. Typically, all were dressed in farm work clothes, but some days, Gonzalo was all dressed up to go to meetings, likely with Mr. Marcus the attorney or to court. He would don his best suit and tie, looking extremely professional, like a feature-movie star of the 1940s. Aki said, "My sister and I thought Gonzalo was *so* tall and handsome in his suit!" Who wouldn't, seeing the transformation from dusty farm clothes to Gonzalo's well-tailored attire, topped with a dashing hat!

*Kindness is...seeing other people uniquely,
without the blinders of racism.*

The Munemitsu family was back home at the Westminster farm, but Seima was still seen as a POW parolee, despite his release from the incarceration camp. It was not until receiving a letter from the Immigration and Naturalization Services dated November 30, 1945, that Seima was "released from parole" and no longer had to report to the INS. By this time, Seima had been back in Westminster on his farm for months. His passport issued by his home country of Japan was returned to him too. He used that passport only three more times to travel to Japan. In 1951, Seima sailed by ship to Japan to visit relatives. In 1956, he and Masako took Aki and Kazi for their first visit to Japan by airplane. He made a final trip to Japan by plane in 1961. That would be the last time he visited the home of his youth, Kochi-ken, Japan.

While the Munemitsu family was back in Westminster and beginning to rebuild their lives, the fight against racism and for equal education for the Mendez children and other Mexican students was just getting started.

CHAPTER 16

Mendez, et al. v. Westminster
Trial and Ruling

Maya Angelou once wrote, "You may encounter many defeats, but you must not be defeated. In fact, it may be necessary to encounter the defeats, so you can know who you are, what you can rise from, how you can still come out of it." This was definitely the attitude Mr. Marcus held while fighting for the children of California.

Just about six months before World War II ended, Attorney Marcus filed the *Mendez, et al. v. Westminster, et al.* class action lawsuit on March 2, 1945, at the US District Court in Los Angeles. As members of a class action lawsuit, the five families were speaking up on behalf of about 5,000 other persons of Mexican descent, citizens and residents of the four school districts of Westminster, Santa Ana, Garden Grove, and El Modena.

The case was assigned to Judge Paul J. McCormick (1879–1960). He was born in New York City, but in 1887 moved to California, where he attended public school. After college and law school, he had a private law practice and was a deputy district attorney. He was named to the California Superior Court to fill a vacancy by the state governor initially, then was elected and reelected, serving thirteen years hearing civil, criminal, and probate cases. In 1924, he was appointed by President Calvin

Coolidge to the US District Court for the Southern District, where he served until 1951. By all measures, Judge McCormick had an impressive resume.

Judge McCormick and his wife were active in the community and in charitable organizations, particularly Catholic charities in the Los Angeles area. "McCormick's strong moral streak and the importance he placed on religion were reflected in his decisions," notes Strum.[36] In her research, Strum concluded, "The jurist [McCormick] who would hear the *Mendez* case, then, was a stern moralist, someone whose feelings about racial differences were mixed at best, a man of stature in his community and in judicial circles generally, a firm believer in the Constitution, and by all accounts, a very pleasant person."[37]

After much legal research, Attorney Marcus decided not to go to the California state court system, but instead filed the case at the federal court level. California education law already permitted segregation of Indian and Asian students. If he filed at the state level, he feared California's government might just add Mexican students to this list, defeating any hopes for desegregation. In his research, he also found other southwestern US states imposing the same type of segregation on Mexican students. If he filed the case in the California state court, it would not have a future impact on national education laws.

All this influenced Marcus to take the case through the federal court system which consists of three levels: the district court, then the Ninth Circuit Court of Appeals—which covers the western states of California, Oregon, Washington, Arizona, Montana, Idaho, Nevada, Alaska, Hawaii, as well as Guam and the Northern Mariana Islands—and, finally, the US Supreme Court in Washington, D.C.

---

36 Strum, *Mendez v. Westminster*, 65-66.

37 Strum, *Mendez v. Westminster*, 67.

Marcus knew that making it a case about race would not be successful. *Plessy v. Ferguson*[38] (1896), *Hirabayashi v. U.S.* (1943), and *Korematsu v. U.S.* (1944) were all examples of how unreliable the US Supreme Court was when it came to ruling in favor of various minority citizens. The Supreme Court's decision about the Japanese American "internment" in *Ex Parte Endo* (1944) was one of the few examples of the Supreme Court ruling in favor of a minority citizen, yet in *Korematsu* the same issue of Japanese American incarceration was, on the same day, ruled lawful given military threats. This made it obvious that the Supreme Court was conflicted in ruling against the government in cases based on race.

Rather than making this an issue of race, Marcus decided to focus on citizenship and the fact that young citizens of Mexican heritage were not equally treated, as they were forced to attend inferior schools with substandard curricula and books. He also argued that segregation based on nationality violated the equal protection clause in the US Constitution's Fourteenth Amendment, which states, "No State shall...deny to any person within its jurisdiction the equal protection of the law." Additionally, the amendment goes on to state, "No State shall make or enforce any law which shall abridge the privileges and immunities of citizens of the United States." The school segregation of Mexican children by these school districts equated to them denying these students "equal protection" and "the privileges" afforded other citizens.

---

38 *Plessy v. Ferguson* is the 1896 US Supreme Court decision that upheld that "separate but equal" is constitutional in public facilities, i.e., it affirmed racial segregation as long as the facilities were equal in quality.

Mrs. Lovell's third grade class of integrated White and Japanese American students at Westminster's Seventeenth Street School in October 1931. Tad Munemitsu proudly stands with a wide grin in overalls in the back row, just to the right of the open doors, in front of the brick wall. This is the same school that the Mendez children were denied enrollment in twelve years later, in Fall 1943.

A class of all Mexican children at Hoover School, 1944, with their first-grade teacher, Mrs. Alice Johnson, showing the segregation of schools in Westminster based on color and race in the 1920s-1940s.
Courtesy of the Mendez family.

The defense for the school districts was provided by George F. Holden, deputy county counsel. Attorney Holden also had vast experience in private practice, as a city judge, and as Orange County district attorney. Notably, he hired Orange County's first female deputy district attorney in October 1942, which was quite progressive for the times. He lost his next election as district attorney, worked as a corporate attorney briefly, and rejoined the government as a deputy district attorney at the time of *Mendez*.

He was a formidable defense attorney at age forty-eight, facing his court opponent, forty-one-year-old David Marcus.[39]

Holden argued, first of all, that local education was a state matter, outside of federal court jurisdiction. The defense attorney representing the school districts claimed that the segregated "Mexican" schools were of equal educational quality and allowed for Mexican students to improve their English language before later immersion with English-speaking students. In this, he attempted to make the case that schools were not segregated solely based on ethnicity, but on English proficiency. Holden tried to strongly prove that the school districts were within their constitutional rights because the school facilities were of "equal" quality.

To win this case, Attorney Marcus had to prove two key points: 1) Based on the Fourteenth Amendment, Mexican American students were being "denied the equal protection of the laws," and 2) segregating the students into separate "Mexican" schools was not providing an equal, but in fact an inferior, quality of education to the young Mexican American citizens.

As the trial went on, Sylvia, at the time a nine-year-old, remembers being really nervous as she sat day after day in the courtroom, worried that she would have to testify. But she never was called to testify and that was a great relief to her. Her mother, Felicitas, did testify though, and she did so with these words:

> We always tell our children they are Americans, and I feel I am American myself, and so is my husband, and we thought that they shouldn't be segregated like that, they shouldn't be treated the way they are. So we thought we were doing the right thing and just asking for the right thing, to put our children together with the rest of the children there.[40]

39 Strum, *Mendez v. Westminster*, pg 68-69.
40 Strum, *Mendez v. Westminster*, 102.

Sylvia Mendez at age ten—around the time of the trials.
Courtesy of the Mendez family.

The five-day trial lasted from July 5 through July 11, 1945, with all five plaintiff families—parents and children—involved. They were not the first to challenge educational segregation in the courts. Would *Mendez, et al. v. Westminster* become the case that would desegregate Orange County school districts and integrate all students? Could *Mendez* initiate the desegregation of all California schools for future generations? Judge McCormick's ruling would not come for seven more months, because he decided to take time to study and review the case.

On February 18, 1946, US District Judge McCormick ruled that "segregation prevalent in the defendant school districts foster antagonisms in the children and suggest inferiority among them where none exists." Further, he ruled that the equal protection clause had been violated by the school districts. In his decision, Judge McCormick also wrote: [t]he equal protection of the laws pertaining to the public school system in California is not provided by furnishing in separate schools the same technical facilities, textbooks and courses of instruction to children of Mexican ancestry that are available to the other public school children regardless of their ancestry. ...A paramount requisite in the American system of public education is social equality. It must be open to all children by unified school association regardless of lineage.[41]

Essentially, Judge McCormick ruled that segregation of students was not equal, just, or lawful. Strum put it this way:

He held that Mexican-Americans as a group were protected by the Fourteenth Amendment and could not legitimately be discriminated against—a holding that would not be echoed by the U.S. Supreme Court until 1954. He declared that school segregation impeded learning instead of enhancing it. ...Most important, of course, he declared that separate but equal education was a violation of the Fourteenth Amendment. There again, he anticipated the Supreme Court by almost a decade.[42]

Kindness is...courage to stand for
what is fair and just for all.

41 Strum, *Mendez v. Westminster*, 125.
42 Strum, *Mendez v. Westminster*, 127.

After Judge McCormick ruled that "separate is not equal," the Westminster School District didn't wait for the appeal process to integrate their schools. The district allowed all the Mexican children, including the Mendez and Vidaurri cousins, to go to the Seventeenth Street School.

Sylvia recalls what a beautiful school it was! It had a library and a wonderful playground. The Munemitsu farm was actually in a White area of Westminster. The Mendez kids rode the same bus they always had: the one that came to a stop on Edwards Street to pick them up each morning, at the dirt road leading to the farm. That bus was full of the friends they played with—White children who already attended Westminster School. But now, at last, they would all be able to walk into the same school once they exited the bus.

Though it's a routine event that happens every year, to have their school class pictures taken at Westminster Seventeenth Street School with all their friends, White and Mexican, was a proud moment for Sylvia, Gonzalo Jr., and Jerome. Together with their friends, they had played on the farm; and now together with their friends, they could attend the same school, go to the same classes, and be in the same class picture. How good it was to be included and together.

Kindness is...including others and being included.

Many ask whether there was any trouble or discrimination against the Mexican children when the school was integrated.

Amazingly enough, because they had already built friendships on the farm, most of the children got along great. Sylvia does remember a boy once telling her, "You're a Mexican. You don't belong here." Though this was hurtful, Sylvia knew she did belong in that school. The federal district court had ruled so, but that did not mean the prejudice in the hearts of adults and children automatically was wiped away. For the most part though, Sylvia remembers the Mexican children at Westminster's Seventeenth Street School were accepted by their White classmates and vice versa. As far as she recalls, there were no cases of widespread violence in the integration of the Mexican children into the formerly White schools in Orange County.

This is a great example of friendships regardless of race, color, or cultural differences. It was the school districts and adminis-trations that had a problem with integrating the schools, not the children. They saw each other as friends and peers from the very beginning. How the innocent wisdom and kindness of children can teach our world so much!

· · · · · · · · · · · ·

One of the unexpected issues in the integration of the Mexican children at Seventeenth Street School was that there was not enough classroom space for all the children at every grade. The decision was made that all the older students, White and Mexican, would go to the Hoover School, formerly the all-Mexican school. Younger students all stayed at Westminster. This surely didn't please the Westminster parents of older students and they complained loudly because now their students had to endure the horrible conditions of the Hoover School facilities.

Sylvia remembers that at the time the former school superin-tendent, Mr. Peters, was the first to send his daughter, who was White, to Hoover School. He wanted to model the importance of integration for the other parents. By sending his own daughter he helped to make space for all the students and endorsed the integration of Mexican children into Seventeenth Street School. To this day, Sylvia and his daughter are friends on social media—a childhood friendship that endures.

Kindness is...sacrificing for the good of others.

Eventually, to resolve the conflict, the school district shut down Hoover School and added classroom space for all the students to stay at Seventeenth Street School, ending the era of "Mexican" school segregation in Westminster.

This made local news, but a much bigger story against systemic racism was just about to make the national headlines.

CHAPTER 17

Running the Bases for Equality

The battle for equal opportunity for all was not just being fought in the area of school desegregation. Indeed, there were a number of fronts to this battle for equality and desegregation—fronts that covered all aspects of American life. On April 15, 1947, Jackie Robinson moved up from the Montreal Royals (Dodgers farm team) to the Brooklyn Dodgers as a Major League first baseman. Most players would make headlines in the Major League based on their athletic performance as the season progressed, not immediately on the day they moved up from the farm team. But not so for Jackie Robinson, who was the first Black/African American player to take the field in baseball's Major League.

Robinson (1919–1972) overcame so many challenges in his life, and he succeeded in changing not only professional baseball, but also hitting hard against the prejudice and discrimination based on color in the 1930s and 40s. Baseball wasn't the only time Jackie endured racism.

Jackie was one of five children raised by a single mother, and theirs was the only Black family on their block—racial prejudice was right next door. Jackie had a successful college career as the first person to earn varsity letters in four sports at UCLA in a single year: he lettered in baseball, basketball, football, and track. Unfortunately, due to finances, he had to leave college and enlist in the US Army. Even while serving his country as a second lieutenant, Jackie endured discrimination because of his race, which led to court-martial proceedings. He eventually left the Army with an honorable discharge.[43]

Jackie returned to the game he loved best, baseball, and was talented enough to draw the attention of some Major League scouts. Though the game of baseball is played on the field, the breaking of the color barrier started at the team headquarters. Branch Rickey, the Brooklyn Dodgers general manager, was impressed with Jackie not only because of his talent on the playing field, but also because of his fortitude, both mentally and emotionally.[44]

Rickey knew that in order to break down the color barrier in baseball, Robinson would need all the support Rickey could give him. Despite Branch's support, Jackie would have to endure and persevere through the very personal abuses, threats, and discrimination that came his way as the only Black man in baseball. His own teammates, opposing teams, baseball fans, and the media were relentless in their criticism and obscenities. He and his family were confronted daily with this difficult reality. But Rickey believed in Robinson and knew he had the chance to make US history, impacting countless lives and making a major impact against racism. Rickey once said, "Problems are the price you pay for progress."

Kindness is...standing together to fight against racism, no matter how difficult it gets.

---

43 https://www.jackierobinson.com.
44 "Jackie Robinson," https://baseballhall.org/hall-of-famers/robinson-jackie.

History would have been so different if Jackie Robinson had given up early. If he, being a member of the only Black family in the neighborhood, believed that he could not overcome discrimination. If he let not having enough money to finish college, or the racism leading to his honorable discharge from the Army, hold him back from fighting for change. Imagine if Jackie had quit after experiencing all that toxic abuse on the baseball field. What would the shape of our country have been?

But Jackie preserved against all odds, with Branch Rickey by his side. He modeled perfectly—though unknowingly—the Japanese gambatte spirit of *never give up*—even if he never heard the word itself.

Jackie once said, "A life is not important except in the impact it has on other lives."[45] Jackie lived his life well indeed.

Kindness is...standing up for those being oppressed because we are one human race.

Among Jackie's many achievements, he was inducted into the Baseball Hall of Fame in 1962.[46] Each baseball season on April 15—the day Jackie entered the Major League in 1947—every Major League team celebrates Jackie Robinson Day by having every player wear his number forty-two jersey, a number that is retired league-wide the rest of the season. This celebration of Jackie Robinson would have seemed a far-off dream on April

45 https://www.jackierobinson.com.

46 "Jackie Robinson," https://baseballhall.org/hall-of-famers/robinson-jackie.

15, 1947, but seeds of justice were being planted on that spring day in Brooklyn.

Across the country, in San Francisco, California, a much smaller headline made the news just the day before Jackie's big-league debut. While the country was all talking about Robinson's historic jump to the Major League, the Ninth Circuit Court of Appeals judges made their final decision on the appeal of *Mendez, et al. v. Westminster* on April 14, 1947. Would this be another step forward in the fight against racial inequality?

CHAPTER 18

The Court Appeal and
1947 Final Ruling

Three of the defending Orange County school districts—all but Westminster—appealed the court ruling of *Mendez, et al. v. Westminster*, asking a higher court to review and rule on the decision, expecting a reversal of Judge McCormick's decision. This appeal sent the case to the Court of Appeals and prolonged the final statewide ruling for over a year, until the spring of 1947.

During the court of appeals process, in the fall of 1946, after the farm lease ended,[47] the Mendez family moved back to their home in Santa Ana. Unlike the Westminster school district, the Santa Ana school district was not willing to let the Mendez children attend the White Franklin school, despite the outcome of the first trial. Sylvia and her brothers went back to Fremont School in the barrio, which felt like a major setback for Gonzalo and the families who had fought so hard for this case. Sylvia and her brothers had already attended the integrated Westminster school for about a year.

For the appeal trial, David Marcus had new allies who voiced their support for the students, each writing and submitting an *amicus* brief—"amicus" being a shortened version of the Latin term *amicus curiae*, meaning *friend of the court*—to the court of

---

47 The farm lease ended on August 31, 1946.

appeals. Each document showed support for the *Mendez* cause. This Westminster, California, case now had national attention as the briefs came in from The American Civil Liberties Union (ACLU), The American Jewish Congress, The Japanese American Citizens League (JACL), the attorney general of California, and the National Association for the Advancement of Colored People (NAACP). Two young lawyers, Robert L. Carter and Thurgood Marshall, penned the brief for the NAACP (Marshall played a support role to Carter in the writing). Both became prominent in the Civil Rights Movement and renown court judges. Robert Carter was nominated by President Richard Nixon to be the US district judge in New York in 1972, while Thurgood Marshall became the first Black justice of the Supreme Court, nominated by President Lyndon B. Johnson in 1967.

Kindness is...looking beyond your own race
in order to look out for others as well.

Finally, the federal court ruling was upheld by a unanimous 7-0 decision by the Ninth Circuit Court of Appeals in San Francisco on April 14, 1947, siding with the Mendez family and all Mexican American children. The court stated:

By enforcing the segregation of school children of Mexican descent against their will and contrary to the laws of California, respondents [the school districts] have violated the federal law as provided in the Fourteenth Amendment to the Federal Constitution by depriving them of liberty and property without due process of law and by denying to them the equal protection of the laws.[48]

The school districts did not appeal this verdict to the US Supreme Court, making this the final ruling on the *Mendez, et al. vs. Westminster* case. This ruling paved the way for California schools to overturn laws of segregation in public school districts.

The Anderson Bill of 1947 was adopted by the state legislature, signed by California governor Earl Warren (1891–1974), and it repealed all California school codes mandating segregation by race. Earl Warren would go on to become the chief justice of the US Supreme Court and rule to end school segregation nationwide with the highest court's decision in *Brown v. Board of Education* (Topeka, Kansas) in 1954, seven years after *Mendez*.

Judge Frederick Aguirre, Superior Court of California, County of Orange, wrote a synopsis of how *Mendez, et al. v. Westminster* set a state precedent. Seven years later, in 1954, the US Supreme Court would rule on *Brown v. Board of Education*, setting a national standard. Judge Aguirre's research notes what the *Mendez* case initiated:

1. Caused the desegregation of public schools in the Southwest for Mexican-American students.
2. Caused the California Legislature, through Governor Earl Warren, to repeal the rest of the segregation laws on the books regarding forced segregation of Asian and Native American children in separate public schools.
3. Caused cities and counties across the Southwest to end practices of segregation in public facilities like parks,

---

48 Judge Frederick P. Aguirre, "Synopsis of *Mendez v. Westminster, et al.*" Also see *Westminster School Dist. of Orange County, et al. v. Mendez, et al.* No. 11310, Circuit Court of Appeals, Ninth Circuit, April 14, 1947, Document 161 F.2d 774 (1947).

pools, theaters, then private places like restaurants, motels, theaters.

4. Set the stage for *Brown v. Board of Education* where Supreme Court Justice Earl Warren would lead the Supreme Court, through the strong legal and moral arguments of the same legal teams that participated in the *Mendez* case, to end segregation in public schools for the entire nation.[49]

Then and now, racial prejudice is a very complex issue. Supreme Court chief justice Earl Warren would go down in history as helping to end school segregation nationally with the court's decision on *Brown v. Board of Education*. This would lead to the assumption that he accepted all people equally and justly throughout his life in public office. Yet, as attorney general of California during World War II, Earl Warren supported the racial prejudice and unjust incarceration of Japanese American residents and citizens. This illustrates just how complex the issues of discrimination and prejudice are. Deep roots of prejudice and racism are not easily changed and may even contradict situationally, especially in times of war when fear rules.

It wasn't until after retiring from the Supreme Court that Warren started to write his memoirs. These memoirs, published in 1977, three years after his death, revealed that he had "since deeply regretted the removal order and my own testimony advocating it, because it was not in keeping with our American concept of freedom and the rights of citizens. ...When I thought of the innocent little children who were torn from home, school friends, and congenial surroundings, I was conscience-stricken." At the

---

49 Judge Frederick Aguirre, 2.

end of his life, Warren believed that "[i]t was wrong to react so impulsively, without positive evidence of disloyalty..."[50]

Kindness is...humbly admitting you made a mistake, even though years have passed.

Some people would argue that, in time of war, the incarceration of the Japanese American citizens and residents was necessary for national security. Yet, not every German and Italian immigrant or citizen of White ancestry was identified as a potential spy and accused of possible treason, nor were such citizens incarcerated on a wide scale. Germany had not physically attacked US soil, but, as made apparent by the millions killed by Hitler's forces, it cannot be denied that Germany was after supreme rule as a world power. The Nazi regime was a definite threat to freedom where it existed.

No evidence was ever found that any of the 120,000 Japanese American citizens or residents incarcerated in World War II were guilty of any malice or treason to the United States. None. If American citizens are innocent, law-abiding citizens, why should the color of their skin make a difference in how they are treated? What fears reside so deeply that we treat innocent neighbors differently because of the color of their skin?

. . . .

50 G. Edward White, "The Unacknowledged Lesson: Earl Warren and the Japanese Relocation Controversy," VQR, Autumn 1979, https://www.vqronline.org/essay/unacknowledged-lesson-earl-warren-and-japanese-relocation-controversy.

From the money made on the Munemitsu farm, Gonzalo was able to buy another cantina, The Mendez Cafe, on Beach and Katella, in nearby Midway City, just north of Westminster. He now knew many people in Westminster and chose to start his new business there at a leased restaurant site, even though his family had already moved back to their home in Santa Ana. The new Mendez Cafe did well and it looked to be another successful business owned by Gonzalo.

Unfortunately, it was only a few years before Beach Boulevard was widened and, through the eminent domain process, the land was taken for the road expansion. Because he did not own the land, Gonzalo was not compensated at all, and he had to close the business he had built in the rented restaurant space. He brought all the restaurant equipment he had back to their Santa Ana home to start over again.

Gonzalo was a man of perseverance with an entrepreneurial spirit. He didn't give up and founded another cantina, The Palms, in rented space at First and Grand, in Santa Ana. Sadly, a few years later, First Street was also widened, the land taken, and the cantina was closed. Gonzalo lost yet another cantina he had worked so hard to establish. While the building and land owner was meagerly compensated for the land taken, as a renter Gonzalo was not compensated and just had to close his business again.

Sylvia says that, after that, business for the family was difficult. She recalls how horrible those days were for her parents, especially her father. While he and others had fought and unselfishly sacrificed for the children of California to go to the public schools, circumstances outside his control were the demise of his next two restaurants.

*Kindness is...persevering for what you
believe without thought of any reward.*

Yet the legacy of Gonzalo and Felicitas Mendez is more than
that of successful cafe owners or farmers. They modeled hard
work as entrepreneurs. They went after their dreams to farm and
showed great integrity in leasing the Munemitsu farm during
the incarceration. They rallied their community to fight against
injustice peacefully, thinking not only of their children, but of
all the children in such unfair circumstances. They did the right
things and persevered despite the odds against them. They are
American heroes. As Christopher Reeve once said, "I think a
hero is an ordinary individual who finds strength to persevere
and endure in spite of overwhelming obstacles."

CHAPTER 19

Poston's Next Unexpected Residents

On one family trip to the Grand Canyon in the 1960s, we visited Poston. I was surprised to see how well-paved the roads were and to see the extensive fields of grains, cotton, lettuce, and other leafy greens that lay on either side of the road. My dad said these were "corporate" farms, land leased from Native American reservations. He remembered Poston internees figuring out how to farm and cultivate crops in what was thought to be a desert wasteland.

The dome-shaped auditorium was still standing, but not much else. My parents, from memory, tried to outline what the camp once looked like based on the location of that one landmark. There was no formal sign or memorial in those days, but their memories set up our own landmark of sorts—what had once been and how thankful we were that it was over.

On February 16 through 17, 1985, my parents got another chance to visit Poston as they attended the Poston Homecoming Weekend. Initiated by the Native Americans of the Colorado River Tribes, the American Baptist Church, and the Poston Community Baptist Church, 275 former Poston internees, family and friends from six US states and Canada, gathered for a most unusual reunion: a reunion of two cultures meeting for the first time, connected by a desert of history and hardship. No, the Native Americans didn't know the Japanese American families back in 1942. No, they didn't all even share the desolate desert

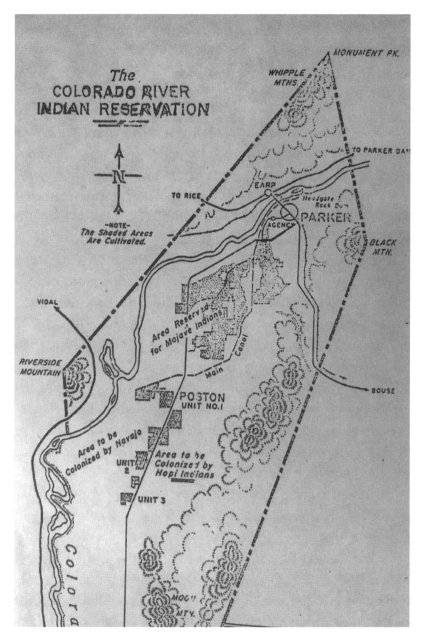

Map of Colorado River Indian Reservation. The Poston unit 1, 2, 3 designations outline the Japanese American incarceration camps of WWII. Poston is thirty-three miles north of Blythe, California, on the Mohave Road, thirty-nine miles southwest of Parker Dam, Arizona, and fifty-three miles south of Lake Havasu City, Arizona, along the California-Arizona state border and the Colorado River.

at the same time. While the Poston camp is the past, these tribes were the present and the future of Poston.

One of the stories shared during that reunion was of sixteen Native American families of the Hopi tribe who arrived in Poston in early September of 1945. They had been relocated by the Bureau of Indian Affairs from their reservation in northeastern Arizona. After hours on buses in the hot Colorado River desert, the caravan stopped and they were told to "go and find a house for yourself." They had arrived at a block of recently deserted barracks that the Japanese, just weeks before, had vacated to go home!

They didn't know what to expect when they arrived, but they "saw the beautiful deserted 'homes' graced by gardens of lush green, fishponds with goldfish living in them, beautiful small bridges spanning the small areas of water, and all the other colorful and homey, ingenious ways a hot merciless desert had been transformed into a meaningful productive land of beauty and faith," recounted a Hopi woman. "We had very little in the way of possessions, so we went around to the empty barracks and thankfully gathered up any items of household goods left by the departing Japanese. One thing we were especially thankful for was the swimming pool left behind..."[51]

Another Hopi shared, "If it hadn't been for you Japanese people who figured out how to condition the soil in this valley and how to farm this land successfully, we wouldn't be here today!"

What the Japanese Americans left in the desert became the beginnings for these Native Americans, who now warmly welcomed the Japanese Americans back to a homecoming of sorts. It was a reunion of fellow internees and those from the Native American community who followed them. My parents talked about experiencing this reunion with their old friends,

---

51 "Poston Pilgrimage: A Celebration in the Desert," *Tozai Times*, April 1985.

making new friends, and the warm hospitality of the Native Americans and Poston Community Baptist Church. Since fellowship and food go together, the food they were served for every meal of the reunion was outstanding!

My mom, Yone, said, "We ate this most delicious thing! I've never seen anything like it before! It was sort of flat and puffy, sweetened with honey, and served hot! It was so delicious, but I don't know what it's called."

"Mom, I think that is Navajo frybread. Homemade, it sounds amazing!" I replied.

Mom, lovingly remembering the ladies who made it, said, "Well, it was the best thing, handmade by the ladies at the church. They made all the meals for us, for everyone. Everything was so delicious. But that frybread was so good. We couldn't stop eating it."

I'm sure it was delicious, but sweeter still was their thoughtfulness in welcoming back the Japanese Americans incarcerated at Poston, and the hospitality shown by Native American strangers, whose families for generations have suffered far worse. The Native Americans remembered and honored the Japanese, had compassion for and welcomed the Poston internees "back home." For my mom, this was better than anything they could make in a kitchen—though the homemade Navajo frybread was amazing!

Kindness is...remembering what others have suffered with compassion and hospitality, even when you have suffered far worse.

I wanted to learn more about the Native Americans now living in Poston, so I found a film series in which tribal leaders of the Colorado River Indian Tribes (CRIT) share about how the World War II incarceration of the Japanese Americans in Poston had a lasting effect on the CRIT people. The Native Americans could truly relate to the Japanese Americans' forced mass relocation, as they too, as a people, were forced, over many decades, to move from their native land to reservations in less desirable locations.

17,814 Japanese Americans were incarcerated at Poston, Arizona. This tribute monument is at the Japanese American Memorial to Patriotism During World War II, National Mall, Washington, DC. A marker for each of the ten camps as well as a memorial to the Japanese Americans who patriotically served and fought in WWII are part of this park just northwest of the US Capitol building.

After the Japanese Americans left Poston in 1945, some recalled how the long wooden barracks were turned over to the tribe as homes, though some were cut into sections for smaller homes and relocated to different areas. They remembered the Japanese fishpond and the vegetable and flower gardens. The infrastructure that was built through three and a half years of hard work by the Japanese Americans gave the Native Americans school buildings, roads, irrigation, and electricity at the center of the reservation.[52]

In 1992, the CRIT Tribal Council allotted forty acres to preserve Poston history and, together with funding raised by the Japanese American-led Poston Memorial Monument Committee and Poston Community Alliance, dedicated the Poston Memorial Monument. This commemorated fifty years since the evacuation and incarceration in 1942. The single thirty-foot concrete pillar of the monument symbolizes "unity of spirit" and the hexagon-shaped base resembles a Japanese stone lantern.[53] Two very different histories and cultures come to a crossroads in Poston, with mutual respect and collaboration for their unique stories that this land shares.

Kindness is...respecting our differences, celebrating shared history, and moving forward as one humanity.

---

52 The film *In Our Voice: The Chemehuevi, Hopi & Navajo Perspectives* (2018), fifty-five minutes long, describes how four tribes came together on the CRIT reservation, and what a Japanese-American internment camp had to do with it. Online source: www.critfilms.org.

53 https://www.postonpreservation.org.

CHAPTER 20

An Apology from the US Government

Change is a process, one that seems to be continuous in our lives, but it does not always come quickly. And change that includes an apology for an unjustified incarceration—and government laws still based on racism—takes even longer to come. Though they were free to return to their homes and were now outside the barbed wire fences of the camps, individuals born in Japan were still not allowed to become naturalized US citizens until 1952. This is just one example of how persistent prejudice and racism are, and of the fact that "liberty and justice for all" was still out of reach.

Through persistent lobbying over the course of many years by the Japanese American community and other allies for justice, progress was made on February 16, 1976, when President Gerald Ford formally rescinded Executive Order 9066, a long thirty-four years after WWII ended. On February 19, 1976, President Ford wrote,

> We now know what we should have known then—not only was that evacuation wrong but Japanese-Americans were and are loyal Americans. On the battlefield and at home the names of Japanese-Americans...have been and continue to be written in our history for the sacrifices and the contributions

they have made to the well-being and to the security of this, our common Nation.[54]

Now the issue was on a national platform, and in 1980 President Jimmy Carter signed legislation to create the Commission on Wartime Relocation and Internment of Civilians (CWRIC), appointed to study Executive Order 9066 and other related wartime orders, in order to discern their impact on Japanese Americans in the West. Two years later, in December 1982, the findings concluded, in *Personal Justice Denied,* the 467-page report of the CWRIC, that the decision to incarcerate was not justified by military necessity but rather on "race prejudice, war hysteria, and a failure of political leadership."

The commission recommended an official government apology and redress payments of $20,000 to each of the survivors and a public-education fund to increase awareness and ensure that this would not happen again. The recommended redress of $20,000 in 1990 was roughly $2,823.16 in 1945 dollars, an amount calculated by the CWRIC for the reimbursement of the inflicted loss of businesses, livelihoods, homes, and three years— losses suffered by the Japanese Americans interned during WWII.

On August 10, 1988, the Civil Liberties Act of 1988, based on the CWRIC recommendations to grant redress payments, was signed into law by President Ronald Reagan. On November 21, 1989, President George H. W. Bush signed an appropriation bill authorizing payments to be paid out over eight years, 1990 to 1998. In 1990, nearly forty-five years after the incarceration camps closed, surviving Japanese American internees began to receive individual redress payments and letters of apology.

54 "Righting a Wrong: Japanese Americans and World War II," subsection "Taking Action," document "An American Promise by the President of the United States of America, A Proclamation," https://americanhistory.si.edu/righting-wrong-japanese-americans-and-world-war-ii.

THE WHITE HOUSE
WASHINGTON

A monetary sum and words alone cannot restore lost years or erase painful memories; neither can they fully convey our Nation's resolve to rectify injustice and to uphold the rights of individuals. We can never fully right the wrongs of the past. But we can take a clear stand for justice and recognize that serious injustices were done to Japanese Americans during World War II.

In enacting a law calling for restitution and offering a sincere apology, your fellow Americans have, in a very real sense, renewed their traditional commitment to the ideals of freedom, equality, and justice. You and your family have our best wishes for the future.

Sincerely,

GEORGE BUSH
PRESIDENT OF THE UNITED STATES

OCTOBER 1990

My mom and dad, along with thousands of other surviving Japanese Americans, received this 1990 presidential apology sent from the White House to fellow American citizens of Japanese descent as a belated acknowledgment of the unjust and forced evacuation of 1942.

Receiving the letter of apology meant a lot to my parents, even more than the monetary redress check. Taking photocopies of the checks they each received, they donated them to the Japanese American National Museum (JANM), Los Angeles, California, which opened in 1992. The JANM is dedicated to preserving the history and culture of Japanese Americans, and includes a permanent historical display and archive of "camp days." My parents did not spend the money on themselves because it was more important to them that the true history be told and remembered, in hopes that this would never happen again to any race in America.

Forty-five years and four US presidents later, they had a letter of apology in hand. My parents kept the letters of apology, signed by President Bush, safely in a file for the rest of their lives, along with the stamped and dated envelopes in which they were sent. Apology accepted.

Kindness is...an apology, though long-awaited and contested, given and accepted.

CHAPTER 21

Sylvia's Passion for *Mendez, et al. v. Westminster*

Sylvia went on to graduate from Santa Ana High School[55] in 1955, a school where she was involved in drill team, drama, and G.A.A. (Girls Athletic Association). Her brothers, Gonzalo Jr. and Jerome, also graduated from Santa Ana High School. Gonzalo Jr. used his skills to become a master carpenter while Jerome went on to join the military and served as a paratrooper in the 101st Airborne Division.

Sylvia earned a nursing degree at Orange Coast College and a bachelor's degree at California State University, Los Angeles. She worked as a nurse and then later as assistant nursing director of pediatrics at LA County USC Hospital for thirty-three years. During her career, Sylvia worked in many different units at the hospital, but she was most fulfilled working in pediatrics, where she could help ill children.

Sylvia moved from Santa Ana to buy a large home in Fullerton, California, in 1970. She and her mother would talk often about life on the farm and the days spent fighting for the right for the children to go to public school. This is an important piece of US history—not to mention California and Orange County

---

55 This is the same high school that my aunt Rakumi graduated from in 1942, and that my mom also would have attended and graduated from—had she not been incarcerated in Poston.

history—that was seemingly forgotten. Felicitas felt it so important for all children to know that public education was not to be taken for granted. This opportunity had been fought for so that all children could attend public schools and not be judged as unworthy based on their race. It also crushed Felicitas' spirit that no one seemed to remember the sacrifice Gonzalo gave to fight for this cause. In the later part of her life, Felicitas expressed the desire for one of her children to continue to tell their family's story.

Sylvia Mendez' Santa Ana High School graduation picture.
Courtesy of the Mendez family.

At the consistent urging of Felicitas, Sylvia decided to start sharing the story of *Mendez, et al. v. Westminster* after she retired. She would go to any group or school that would have her to tell the story. She dedicated much of her retirement (and still does) to make this part of history known. It didn't matter if it was a class of second-graders or a class of law students, Sylvia eagerly shared the story of how California was the first state in the nation to end public school segregation by race. She wanted students to be encouraged to study and people to know the legacy her parents taught her: "That we are all individuals; that we are all human beings; that we are all connected together; and that we all have the same rights, the same freedom."

Sadly, there were doubters as pride and competition arose over who really deserved credit for the outcome of the case. Legal groups claimed it wasn't Gonzalo and Felicitas Mendez who initiated and funded the majority of this case, saying their names were just put on the case with the other four families. Other organizations tried to take credit for funding the case to discredit Sylvia's story. Some went so far as to say that she made this story up. Yet Sylvia continued to share the story because she truly believed that today's students of all ages needed to understand history and how Mexican American families fought to make change legally and peacefully. She also wanted to show how normal people can change prejudicial and unjust rules with perseverance and truth.

I didn't know about this conflict at the time as I hadn't even met Sylvia yet. But while I was cleaning old farm files after the passing of my father in 1997, I found the original lease documents signed by my dad, Tad, and Gonzalo Mendez. Thinking these must be important for my family's history, I kept them with the intent of going back and looking at them more closely later. I am so glad that I did! The lease documents officially put the Mendez family in Westminster at the time of the case and helped to verify Sylvia's firsthand account. I also found my dad's IRS tax filing, showing he worked for Gonzalo. These documents cement Sylvia's story as the truth, quelling the harmful competitive spirit of these doubters.

Gonzalo and Felicitas Mendez, and the other four families of Ramirez, Palomino, Guzman, and Estrada, fought and testified in this case, but not just for their children. They did this to fight the injustice all Mexican children faced in these schools, and their efforts ultimately helped to desegregate all California state school districts, seven years before the US Supreme Court ruling of *Brown v. Board of Education* made similar changes on a national level. These families fought and collaborated for justice and, when Judge McCormick gave the final victorious ruling on *Mendez, et al. vs. Westminster* in 1947, they helped to bring "separate is not equal" education to generations of California school children.

As I mentioned earlier, Sylvia, in her retirement, told the story whenever invited to share. When I first met her, she shared how she visited many elementary schools, intermediate schools, high schools, and colleges every year to tell the story. She would drive or, in her later years, have a family member drive her, all over Southern California. And if the school's invitation came with a plane ticket, Sylvia would sacrifice her time to go and share.

"Janice, I do this because the children need to know that someone, my parents and the other families, fought for them to have this education. They cannot take it for granted. I go to inspire them to study and work hard to get ahead," she once said to me.

*Kindness is...giving your own time to
encourage and lift others up.*

Sylvia's words and dedication to inspire students, especially students of Mexican heritage, impresses me greatly. And I wasn't the only one impressed. Sylvia was awarded the Presidential Medal of Freedom on February 15, 2011, by President Barack Obama, for her service in encouraging students to stay in school and value public school education.

Over the years, she has shared with hundreds of schools nationwide the *Mendez, et al. v. Westminster* story and her role as a lead plaintiff in the lawsuit as a young student. The Presidential Medal of Freedom is an award bestowed by the president of the United States to recognize people who have made "an especially meritorious contribution to the security or national interests of the United States, world peace, cultural or other significant public or private endeavors."

Sylvia Mendez wearing the Medal of Freedom she was awarded by President Barack Obama in 2011.
Courtesy of the Mendez family.

How proud Gonzalo and Felicitas would be of Sylvia, now recognized not only locally but at the highest level of the US government! Their heart for education and students certainly continued on in Sylvia. For all the children! ¡Para todos los niños!

CHAPTER 22

Old Glory, Birds, and Frogs Remembered: It's Not Over

Though the "camp days" were over, three years in remote desert incarceration camps had not only taken a physical toll on the Japanese Americans, but also a largely unspoken emotional cost. Freedom is not free—whether it's fought for on the battleground, in the local schools, or under orders in a hot and dusty desert "camp."

I remember that few, if any, of our Japanese American family friends were interested in camping. Tents and campfires were just not their thing. Perhaps it was that farmers, shopkeepers, and gardeners didn't take much vacation—only a few days here and there when they could. It may have been, however, that they had already had their fill of wilderness living in desolate, remote areas in barracks, eating simple "camp" food. The effect of three-plus years of living behind barbed wire fences can't be underestimated.

Once released with their twenty-five dollars to return and reestablish themselves, the Japanese Americans started life all over again. With focus and an unrelenting, unyielding work ethic, they began to rebuild, but most of these survivors never fully processed the trauma and emotional wounds these experiences left. The Japanese, being a more emotionally restrained culture, worked hard and got "back to business" without regard for the emotional toll the incarceration had taken.

With that in mind, I found keepsakes became important clues to their internal struggle to cope with their emotions and be "good" citizens, despite the cruel and unfair reality of their incarceration and loss of freedom. My mom had an affinity for birds, frogs, and American flags, though she never deeply expressed why. After her death, I began to see the connection between my mom's favorite keepsakes and the years spent "in camp."

It wasn't obvious, but my mother saved a lot of American flags—Old Glory in all its glory: printed in the newspaper or magazines, small plastic flag pins, inexpensive metal flag pins, small cloth flags. A guest visiting her house would never really notice anything excessive and neither did I in my lifetime. But as I was cleaning out my parents' home after my mom passed in 2010, I found a desk drawer with American flag stickers of all kinds and flags of all sizes cut out of the newspapers or magazines. She had personally affixed them to pieces of cardboard to save.

The flag known for freedom also flew over the Poston camp. While the flag flew freely, it represented something the residents did not have. But the flag that flew over Poston was still a promise of what the United States of America stands for: freedom. No doubt this had an impact on my mom, Yone, still a teenager in camp, as she longed for the day that freedom would be restored and returned. She had hope in Old Glory, even behind the barbed wire fence."

The cardboard I found these flags on was always valuable for my mom too. I bet you never thought of saving the cardboard from the remnant of a notepad. My mom always did. Cardboard pieces were valuable to plug holes in the plywood boards that made up a camp home. Some good pieces of cardboard could help to keep the bitterly cold winter winds from blowing into the one-room family living unit or the hot, dry summer dust from constantly seeping in.

Rakumi and Yone Sasaki in Poston Arizona, 1943, with US
flagpole in the distance (far right corner of the photo).

My mother continued the habit of saving perfectly good pieces of letter-size cardboard throughout the rest of her life. And because my mom saved good cardboard, I always have too. It comes in handy all the time! For many years, I did not fully realize the significance of this for my mom. Decades later, remnant habits and memories of camp life are still evident.

Another aspect of camp days that my mom seemed to cherish were birds. Birds are everywhere, even in the hot and dusty deserts. For my mom, birds meant life. They sing no matter the situation and, more importantly, could fly freely. I really think that the reason my mom loved birds is because of the hope they brought her in Poston. Birds might have been one of the few things that brought joy on the long days spent facing an uncertain future. She kept a bird-watcher's book of birds and

174

inexpensive bird mementos she found on trips. In addition, Yone and her friends had bird pins, some roughly carved and painted by amateurs, while others were beautifully crafted by our family friends, the Takahashis.

Yone wasn't the only one who saw the joy of birds at Poston. Japanese Americans Yoneguma (Joe) and Kiyoka Takahashi and their family were incarcerated at Poston too. They attended a bird-carving class in camp, led by a fellow internee who shared their hobby to provide some kind of craft-making activity for the community. They learned and excelled at the art of carving and painting bird pins out of leftover wood used to build the camp barracks. They made bird pins in the camp and, even after their release from camp in 1945, they continued to create these pins as home-based entrepreneurs. For forty years, the Takahashis perfected their craft and made it their legacy, a legacy born in "camp days."[56]

Original hand-carved and hand-painted bird pins given to
Yone and Janice by Mr. and Mrs. Takahashi.

56 For more information on the Takahashis' handmade bird pins, see: https://taka-hashibirds.com.

My mom and I received bird pins as gifts from the Takahashis when I was a little girl. They lived nearby and were among a group of our friends. My pin is a bright red cardinal, a Takahashi original, a true treasure of the joy found even in an incarceration camp. I didn't fully appreciate the craftsmanship and artistry of the bird pins then, but now as an adult, I can imagine the delightful freedom the birds signified, beautiful in color and free to fly.

My mom also collected small inexpensive plastic or ceramic frogs. Thinking that they were just cute additions in her garden, I asked why she liked frogs. She answered, "Because frog in Japanese is *kaeru* and *kaeru* also means to return, to come home." As a young child, I didn't think much about it, but when cleaning out her home after her passing, I found many small frogs, here and there. I have no doubt what they meant.

Kaeru reminded my mom of her return home from camp, of things returning to how they once were, back in Santa Ana, California, on the farm her father had started decades before. Frogs were another symbol of hope and faith that the camps were just a temporary, albeit harsh, detour in life. In Japan, this is a play on words as well: frogs are considered a symbol of prosperity, that wealth and fortune will return (kaeru) wherever there is a frog (kaeru). Frogs must have reminded my mom that, indeed, she did get her deepest desire: to return home after the camp. That season of life was over, now a distant memory.

Until, that is, September 11, 2001. On that date, planes were highjacked by terrorists and used as missiles. They crashed them into buildings, and brought America into a new war against terrorism. The attacks on New York's World Trade Center, the Pentagon, and a deadly, detour crash-landing in a field in Pennsylvania took 2,977 innocent lives. In addition, over twenty-five thousand more people—firefighters, police officers, rescue workers, other first responders, and people in the vicinity of the attacks—experienced injuries and lasting health consequences.

This day changed the world forever, and for some, like my mother, it brought back the trauma and painful history of fifty-nine years prior. 9/11 was another attack on America and Americans. It was an attack unlike anything the world had ever known, yet it felt familiar for those who experienced the trauma of the Pearl Harbor attack and those who were wrongfully imprisoned in response.

About a month after 9/11, I was about to leave on a long-planned trip east in October 2001. I would only be gone five days or so, and by that time, travelers were being encouraged to try to get America working again. I didn't feel any anxiety over this trip. It was not a big deal for me, a seasoned traveler. But my mother and aunt were beyond terrified and angry that I would think of leaving on a trip. Living in suburban Orange County wasn't very high risk and their homes were in safe neighborhoods.

"But what if they come take us away and you are not here!" they retorted emotionally. At first, I had no idea what my mom and aunt were getting at. I had not even considered the deep wounds of the past this was bringing up.

"What do you mean 'take you away'?" I asked.

"What if they come to take us away to camp again?" their frightened voices echoed.

My heart sank! Of course—an attack against the US, so many innocent victims, all combined with the news and politicians talking about rounding up any potential terrorists. Citizens and immigrants alike were becoming victims of racial profiling, based on the race of the radical, extremist terrorists. All this talk in the media had taken my mother and aunt back to the time in 1942 when they were eighteen and nineteen years old. They were reliving the horror of Pearl Harbor, racial discrimination, Executive

Order 9066, and being ordered into Poston incarceration camp for an unknown amount of time.

My automatic and naive reply was, "But you are citizens. Born here in the United States. They are talking about people here illegally." Wrong response! In 1942, Yone and Rakumi Sasaki were citizens, born in Santa Ana, California. It didn't matter then where you were born. You looked Japanese, had a Japanese name, and so you were classified as the enemy. They were re-experiencing this trauma fifty-nine years later. It could never be erased from their memories.

Kindness is...understanding that racism can cause deep, painful, and long-lasting wounds in the heart.

This form of PTSD (post-traumatic stress disorder) had been latent for almost six decades, but the similarities of the attack, along with the media and government sound-bites, had taken them back to the fear that history could repeat itself—even if not for them, for other innocent residents who had nothing else in common with the terrorist bombers except for the color of their skin, their nationality, or their country of origin.

The Mendez and the Munemitsu family stories met the same obstacle in different situations: prejudice against us because of the color of our skin and the nationality of our family surnames. These deep, painful wounds do not heal easily. Over half a century later, the trauma and fear roared back with even just the words of a distant voice, on a television screen. But these voices echoed the mantra that the color of the skin indicted you as "the enemy."

Needless to say, I postponed any future trips for months to ease the nerves of my family. I wanted to try to care for the emotional PTSD (post-traumatic stress disorder) wounds of my mom and aunt.

CHAPTER 23

Two Families, Two Colors: Kindness in Common

After the Mendez family left the Westminster farm in 1946, both families went back to working hard, raising families, and making a living.

In 1964, hard work and the disappointment of losing his next two cantinas took a toll on Gonzalo Mendez, both emotionally and physically. He died of heart failure at the rather young age of fifty-one. Felicitas Mendez lived for over thirty years more under Sylvia's loving care. Felicitas passed in 1998 at age eighty-two. They are survived by their children: Sylvia, Gonzalo Jr., Jerome, Sandra, Phillip, and their extended families.

My grandfather Seima Munemitsu continued to farm into the 1970s, but passed in 1978 at age seventy-eight. He lived on US soil for sixty-two years of his life. My grandma Masako lived to age ninety-three, passing in 1997. Earlier that same year, my dad, Tad, a man full of health until skin cancer manifested into brain tumors, passed in 1997, at age seventy-five. They are survived by Saylo, Aki, and Kazi, along with their spouses and extended families, and by me.

Gonzalo Mendez and the Munemitsu family are all buried at Westminster Memorial Park, adding to the legacy and history of what happened because of a small Westminster farm.

Felicitas and Gonzalo Mendez.
Courtesy of the Mendez family.

The Mendez family at the unveiling of the US postage stamp commemorating
Mendez v. Westminster in 2007: Jerome, Sylvia, Sandra, Gonzalo, and Philip Mendez
(left to right). *Courtesy of the Mendez family.*

I don't have many regrets, but it does sadden me that my
dad passed before my family and I were reunited with Sylvia and

her brothers. I think he would have just loved to share in the old stories and recount meeting Gonzalo for the first time. He would have gratefully shared his thanks to the children of Gonzalo and Felicitas for what they did working the farm and running it well in his absence. Unfortunately, it wasn't until 2003, with what, at the time, seemed like a random phone call, that our families reconnected and this story was unearthed.

Father and son, Seima and Tad, continued working side by side until Seima's passing in 1978. Here they hold a spring harvest of strawberries at their Garden Grove, California, farm in the early 1950s.

At the time, director and producer Sandra Robbie was working on producing the award-winning documentary, *Mendez vs. Westminster: For All the Children/Para Todos los Niños*. She decided to find out whose small farm it was that the Mendez family lived on all those years ago. In addition, Sylvia and her brothers wanted to see if they could reconnect with the Munemitsus. Sylvia says, "We wanted to find the family and especially the little girls I played with, but I was only a little girl then and I didn't know how to spell Munemitsu."

Kazi Munemitsu Doi, Saylo Munemitsu, Masako Munemitsu, Aki Munemitsu Nakauchi, and Seiko "Tad" Munemitsu in 1985.

After many calls to local Japanese Americans, one man told her, "Maybe you are spelling it wrong. Maybe you are looking for the Munemitsu family, rather than Munimutsu." This final clue led Sandra to connect with me. It took some prodding, but I finally convinced my aunt Aki, who lived in Westminster at the time, to go with me to meet Sylvia at the taping of the documentary in the fall of 2002.

Sylvia and I are often asked to share the story of *Mendez, et al. v. Westminster*. Each time we tell the story, we are always sure to share about the two families who, despite having different cultures and national origins, were united by their parallel struggle with and perseverance against discrimination, prejudice, and racism.

Perhaps the interest in our interwoven family story stems from it not being just a Mexican American story or a Japanese

American story. Rather, it is the story of people just trying to do the best they could in the face of difficult and unjust situations.

The other commonality our families share is that we were not raised to judge on the basis of someone's skin color. We were raised to treat people with kindness, as much as we imperfect humans are able to do so. This was a high value in our families and with our friends. Gonzalo Mendez had business friends in Santa Ana that lived in both the White and barrio neighborhoods. My dad, Tad, had a White banker, and leased all his earthly belongings to a Mexican American cantina owner.

This picture commemorates the first time I met Sylvia Mendez in September 2002, with my aunt Aki Munemitsu Nakauchi. For Aki and Sylvia (left and center), it was a reunion after over fifty-six years.

Kindness is...respecting people for who they are and not judging them by the color of their skin.

Children too are wonderful examples of kindness regardless of color. It is not until prejudiced and biased adults, institutions, organizations, governments, and cultures instill a racial bias in children that they start to view race as a differentiation and make unfair judgments and decisions based on it.

I never really thought about it before, but I was raised with more Mexican Americans around me than Japanese or White as a child. I lived on the farm with my mom and dad, with my grandma and grandpa's house just across the driveway. It was our family strawberry farm in Garden Grove, which we moved to after the Westminster farm was claimed via eminent domain for the construction of two schools. On the new farm there was a big barn, a loading dock for produce, tractors, trucks, and space galore to explore for insects and cats—when I was not helping with work around the farm.

There was also a workers' house where Jesús and his two adult sons, Antonio and José, lived and worked, and another house closer to my grandma's house, where Zubieta lived. These men had legal green cards to work in the US seasonally, which usually meant about nine to ten months of the year, during the whole strawberry growing and harvesting season, and the summer season of beans and squash, which we raised as interim crops. They returned to Mexico in December, January, and early February. They had families and beautiful homes in Central Mexico, funded by their hard work and the savings they wisely put away. They would proudly show us pictures of their children upon their return each year. I still have a silver sombrero pin they gave me, and other special gifts that they would bring back each year from their homes.

Though I have no brothers or sisters, we always had a full table on Thanksgiving Day with our farm family. My mom, aunt, and I cooked a huge traditional turkey, mashed potatoes, farm-grown green beans, yams, and bought Marie Callender's pumpkin pie, all served on my mom's wedding china. English, Japanese, and Spanish were spoken around the table, and somehow we all understood each other after years of working together. I never saw them as different than me, despite the Spanish language they spoke or different Mexican customs they had. To me, they were Zubieta, Jesús, Antonio, and José, my older friends on the farm and loyal workers to my dad. There was a lot of mutual respect and gratitude around our table as we worked together year after year, season after season.

Kindness is...mutual respect and gratitude for each other.

I am often asked to share what was most important to me about this story and the answer is an insight that still rings true now, more than ever before. There is so much in this world and in this life that we cannot control. We can study hard, work hard, be good citizens, but that doesn't always mean that we control the situations or people we encounter in life—at least not fully. Sometimes we will be met with justice and fairness, and, sadly, we will also sometimes be confronted with injustice and unfair accusations. What we can choose to control is ourselves. We can learn to, and choose to, not put a judgment or value on the color of someone's skin. We can learn to treat each other with kindness, despite different situations, cultures, and languages, without assigning bias or value as better or worse.

Though not perfect people by any means, Gonzalo and Felicitas Mendez, my grandparents and parents, Mr. Monroe, and their friends all wanted to be good neighbors. They wanted to help others as they could, and not treat people differently because of the color of their skin. They worked hard to not presume bias or to discriminate based on someone›s culture, language, or the color of their skin. They chose to work things out and help each other, not motivated by greed or entitlement. They were grateful for each other's friendship, hard work, honesty, and integrity.

I'm struck by how many times in this story an act of kindness made a significant and dramatic difference for others. The collaboration of kindness and neighborly goodwill helped these families in some of the hard times. It was not only the kindness of friends and neighbors, but also it was the kindness of strangers that made a significant difference in their lives. And we too can make that sort of difference in the lives of friends and strangers alike.

Sure, there are many unexpected things in life that disrupt our own plans. Life doesn't always go smoothly, but the power lies in how we respond to these situations, not in the crisis itself. I want to remember that *crisis* written in Japanese means both *danger* and *opportunity*—and so we must look for the opportunity within the trouble. Within every crisis lies an opportunity for kindness.

How then can we be people of kindness in the midst of others' crises? A kind word? An offer of help? A listening ear? A compassionate smile? An act of generosity? There are so many beautiful shades of kindness in us. Let us share the kindness within because, together, we are *The Kindness of Color*.

From Past to Present

A seventeenth-century Dutch philosopher, Baruch Spinoza, is credited with saying, "If you want the present to be different from the past, study the past." I hope, as you study and reflect on the past contained in this book, you are a part of positive change for the future. As this book comes to a close, I've included in this epilogue some of the ways that this story continues to be shared and remembered beyond this book. I encourage you to keep diving into these stories, as they can serve as seeds that grow in your heart and bear the fruit of kindness for generations to come.

. . . .

Often people ask if the Munemitsu farm still exists. My family farmed there until the early 1950s, when the land was appropriated by the city as "eminent domain" for two public schools. Eminent domain refers to the power the government has to take private property and convert it into public use. In this case, the local city government paid for the land, but, as is typical in cases of eminent domain, the price paid was below market value. My aunt Aki remembers that this didn't bother my grandfather or dad too much, and they ended up making a donation to the school library. In some ways, I believe this use of their former property meant a lot to them, as they both placed a high value on education. My dad, Tad, used to say, "Education is one thing no one can take away from you," and he encouraged me in all my schooling and college pursuits.

Munemitsu Farms moved to nearby Garden Grove, and the Finley Elementary and Johnson Intermediate Schools of the Westminster School District were built. The Munemitsu Farm address, 13603 South Edward Street, Westminster, California, is now the address of Johnson Intermediate School,[57] with Finley Elementary next door (13521 Edwards Street). What a fitting statement that the farm has now been home to two integrated, multiethnic schools for decades and generations of immigrant and American-born families!

The farm once owned by Japanese American citizens wrongly accused of disloyalty and spy activity against the US in World War II; the farm situated in a district where Mexican children were rejected at the neighborhood school and sent to a segregated "Mexican" school; *that* farmland is now two schools with credentials of academic excellence for all the children. Yes, for all the children, *para todos los niños*!

. . . .

In the late 1960s, back when the Orange County Courthouse and Civic Center in Santa Ana had been newly constructed, the Japanese American Community Services (JACS) raised over fifty thousand dollars to construct a beautiful Japanese garden and teahouse, with an authentic Japanese-style tiled roof. They planted a fifty-year-old bonsai pine tree in the new Civic Center mall. My father was on the JACS board and was the canvassing chairman, and my grandfather was noted as a JACS Issei advisor.

I remember folding and stamping letters that requested donations for this project. At the time, I didn't think much of it—just another community project my father and other Nisei

---

57 For more on Johnson Intermediate School, see: http://johnson.wsdk8.us/.

family friends were involved in. What strikes me now is that it was dedicated on May 27, 1970, almost exactly twenty-five years to the day they returned to their Orange County homes and farms from "camp." It is notably right next to the Superior Court Central Justice Center. Neither of these facts are coincidence. The plaque reads:

Dedicated and Presented for the Pleasure of All People in Orange County by the Japanese American Community. A Grateful Arigato in Honor of our Pioneer Fathers and for the Blessings of Freedom. May 27, 1970

On November 10, 2020, I was invited to commemorate the fiftieth anniversary of the Orange County Japanese Garden and Teahouse. All socially distanced and in masks, about twenty invited guests gathered to remember this heritage of Japanese Americans in Orange County. Not a word was mentioned about the evacuation, "internment," or dusty dry desert of Poston where most of the Orange County Japanese were interned. The bonsai tree, now 130 years old, thrives humbly in true gambatte Japanese character in the shadow of the eleven-story tower of justice at 700 W. Civic Center Drive, Santa Ana.

. . . .

Over the years, Gonzalo and Felicitas Mendez have been remembered for their leadership in the legal battle of *Mendez, et al. v. Westminster* through the naming of two school campuses: the Gonzalo and Felicitas Mendez Intermediate Fundamental School in Santa Ana Unified School District, dedicated on December 8, 1997; and the Felicitas and Gonzalo Mendez Learning Center, dedicated by the Los Angeles Unified School District in East Los

Angeles in 2009. In addition, the Sylvia Mendez Elementary School was dedicated by the Berkeley Unified School District, in Berkeley, California, on May 24, 2018.

· · · · · · · · · · · ·

In 2003, Sandra Robbie, writer and producer, received an Emmy Award and a Golden Mike for the documentary, *Mendez vs. Westminster: For All the Children/Para Todos los Niños*. As a child, Sandra attended both the elementary and jr. high schools built on the acreage of the former Munemitsu Farm. When she first learned about the story as an adult, she decided to produce a documentary while still an intern at KOCE-TV. This documentary featured Sylvia Mendez and the four families named in the case, bringing the story to film for the first time. This thirty-minute documentary was pivotal in gaining more awareness for *Mendez, et al. v. Westminster*, as it aired on PBS to a very broad audience, and could be shown in schools across the US.

· · · · · · · · · · · ·

To acknowledge the sixtieth anniversary of the case in 2007, the US Postal Service honored the *Mendez, et al. v. Westminster* ruling with a forty-one-cent commemorative stamp titled "Toward Equality in Our Schools. Mendez, et al. v. Westminster 1947."

· · · · · · · · · · · ·

Philippa Strum authored *Mendez v. Westminster: School Desegregation and Mexican-American Rights* in 2010. Published by the University Press of Kansas, this book gives an excellent account of the case and its background. It is a volume in a series of books, *Landmark Law Cases and American Society*.

· · · · · · · · · · · ·

For over twenty years, Sylvia has shared the story of the legal case with thousands of students across the country in her retirement. For her commitment to educational equality for all students, Sylvia Mendez was awarded the Presidential Medal of Freedom, the highest civilian honor in the United States, on February 15, 2011, by President Barack Obama, for her service in encouraging students to stay in school and value public school education by sharing the *Mendez, et al. v. Westminster* story and her role as a lead plaintiff in the lawsuit as a young student.

. . . .

Sylvia & Aki, written by author Winifred Conkling, was published in 2011. For this children's story, Winifred creatively wove together a sweet fictional storyline based on the true story of Sylvia and Aki's childhood friendship. It is a popular book among elementary-age children.

Sylvia & Aki, by Winifred Conkling.

. . . .

When people hear about the *Mendez, et al. v. Westminster* case, they always wonder why this history has never been shared before. A major step forward was taken when the California State Board of Education drafted a history/social science curriculum framework providing teaching standards that included the history about the Mendez case in several grade levels in 2009. It wasn't adopted until 2016, when the State Board of Education adopted a revised version of this framework that included *Mendez, et al. v. Westminster* as recommended content at several grade levels. As students in California study this history, more awareness is building about this important California court case and the national impact it eventually had.

. . . .

The *Mendez, et al. v. Westminster* story was highlighted as a #GoogleDoodle in 2020. On September 15, 2020, Google featured "Celebrating Felicitas Mendez" as the daily #GoogleDoodle as part of the Hispanic Heritage Month celebration.[58]

. . . .

In order to commemorate the seventy-fifth anniversary of the case in 2022, the City of Westminster and the Orange County Department of Education are collaborating to create the Mendez Historic Freedom Trail and Monument. The two-mile-long Freedom Trail along Hoover Street includes a walking path and bike lane, with large, illustrated educational panels outlining the history of equal rights in America. At the corner of Olive and Westminster Blvd., the trail culminates in a gathering place for people of all races, ages, and creeds to come together in

---

58 To see it, go to www.google.com and search for "Felicitas Mendez Google Doodle."

remembrance of *Mendez, et al. v. Westminster*. This exhibit is intended to remind all of us that ordinary people can make a difference when they see an injustice that needs correction. The corner park includes statues of Gonzalo and Felicitas Mendez, by famed sculptor Ignacio Gomez.

The groundbreaking ceremony for the monument was held on October 13, 2020. Members of the Westminster City Council and Dr. Al Mijares, Orange County Superintendent of Schools, used a weathered, old Munemitsu Farms shovel from the mid-1900s at the ceremonial groundbreaking held at the corner of Olive and Westminster Blvd.

Resources for More on the Japanese American Incarceration Camps

Many memoirs, books, and films of note have been created to highlight the Japanese American experience during World War II. These are just some of the great resources, physical sites, and online websites where you can find more information:

- Japanese American National Museum, founded in 1985 to preserve the rich heritage and cultural identity of Japanese Americans. It has an extensive ongoing exhibit, *Common Ground: The Heart of Community*, that covers 130 years of Japanese American history, including the World War II incarceration.
  369 E 1st St, Los Angeles, CA 90012
  www.janm.org

- The Smithsonian Museum in Washington, DC, produced an exhibit in 2017 commemorating the seventy-fifth anniversary of Executive Order 9066. Their website has an overview of the exhibit.
  Go to *www.si.edu* and search "75th Anniversary of Executive Order 9066 (2017)."

- The Japanese American Memorial to Patriotism During World War II is in Washington, DC. Facing the Capitol building, it is to the left side at the triangular intersection of D Street NW, New Jersey Avenue NW, and Louisiana Avenue NW. It honors Japanese Americans who proved their loyalty to the US by persevering in the incarceration camps and serving in the US military during World War II.
  www.njamemorial.org

- The National Park Service oversees three of the former
  incarceration camps as National Historic Sites: Manzanar,
  Minidoka, and Tule Lake.
  *https://www.nps.gov/articles/japanese-american-in-
  ternment-archeology.htm*
  In addition, search for "Confinement and Ethnicity: an
  Overview of World War II Japanese American Relocation
  Sites," by authors J. Burton, M. Farrell, F. Lord, and R.
  Lord, on the nps.gov site, to see more details and pictures
  of every incarceration camp.

- Densho.org is a nonprofit organization that offers extensive
  online resources dedicated to preserving stories of the
  Japanese American incarceration during World War II.
  Densho is a Japanese term meaning "to pass on to the next
  generation"—in essence, to leave a legacy.
  www.densho.org

- The Korematsu Institute provides an excellent video, "Of
  Civil Wrongs and Rights," that presents the history of the
  case *Korematsu v. United States* 1944, as well as the plight
  of the Japanese Americans during World War II. This
  twenty-four-minute video can be found at their website.
  http://www.korematsuinstitute.org or on Vimeo at
  https://vimeo.com/417440821

- The History website provides an overview article on the
  Japanese incarceration.
  *https://www.history.com/topics/world-war-ii/
  japanese-american-relocation*

- <u>Walk the Farm</u> is an online resource of Tanaka Farms, Irvine, California, that features a compilation of the stories of Issei and Nisei farmers along the Pacific coast of the United States in the late 1800s and early 1900s. The Tanakas are longtime farming friends of the Munemitsus. *https://www.walkthefarm.org/jafarms*

Chronology of Key Story Events

1848—Treaty of Guadalupe Hidalgo signed. Mexican-American War ends, establishing the American Southwest as part of the United States.

1869-1893—California enacts laws that permit school districts to segregate Asian and Native American (Indian) students.

1896—The US Supreme Court holds that "separate but equal" public accommodations are constitutional in *Plessy v. Ferguson*.

1899—Seima Munemitsu born in Kochi-Ken, Shikoku, Japan.

1910-1930—During the Mexican Revolution, thousands of Mexicans immigrated yearly to the United States.

1913-1920s—"Mexican" schools are established throughout Southern California.

1913—Gonzalo Mendez born in Chihuahua, Mexico.

1916—Seima Munemitsu immigrated to the US from Japan by ship. He joined his parents, who immigrated earlier. He is seventeen years old.

1916—Felicitas Gomez (Mendez) born in Juncos, Puerto Rico.

1918—Seima Munemitsu registered for World War I military service draft in the United States, but was never called to service.

1919—Gonzalo Mendez and his family come to the US (Gonzalo is seven years old).

1921—Seima returns to Japan and marries Masako Morioka. They return to the US by ship and settle in the Torrance, California, area.

1922—Seiko Lincoln Munemitsu is born in Torrance; he is Seima and Masako's first child, an American citizen.

1923—A second son, Saylo, was born to Seima and Masako Munemitsu in 1923.

1926—Felicitas Gomez (Mendez) and her family come to the US from Puerto Rico, an American territory, as American citizens.

1929-1939—The Great Depression.

1931—Munemitsu Family moves from Torrance to farm in Westminster, California.

1935—Gonzalo and Felicitas Mendez are married.

1935—Akiko Munemitsu and her twin sister, Kazuko, are born to Seima and Masako.

1936—Sylvia Mendez is born as the eldest child of Gonzalo and Felicitas.

1939-1945—World War II.

1940-45—Mexican American parents in Westminster, Garden Grove, Santa Ana, and El Modena have issues with segregated schools and voice their concern to the school boards. No changes are made in response to their requests.

December 7, 1941—Pearl Harbor, Hawaii, is bombed by Imperial Japan.

1941-1945—Both Mexican American and Japanese American soldiers serve in US military during World War II.

February 19, 1942—Executive Order 9066 signed by President Roosevelt.

May 14, 1942—Seima Munemitsu arrested and accused of being a spy for Imperial Japan.

May 17, 1942—Masako and the rest of the Munemitsu family relocated to Poston incarceration camp.

Spring 1944—The Mendez family moves to the Munemitsu home and farm in Westminster.

September 1944—The Mendez children are not allowed to enroll at Westminster's Seventeenth Street School, where the Munemitsu daughters went prior to the incarceration and also where the Mendez' cousins, the Vidaurris, are allowed to enroll, but will not unless their Mendez cousins can too.

December 18, 1944—US Supreme Court decision on two cases: *Ex Parte Mitsuye Endo* (ruled in favor of Endo) and *Korematsu v. U.S.* (ruled against Korematsu).

March 2, 1945—Attorney David Marcus files *Mendez, et al. v. Westminster, et al.* in federal district court.

July 5-11, 1945—Trial, with Judge Paul McCormick presiding.

September 2, 1945—World War II officially ends.

September 1945—Munemitsu family leaves the Poston incarceration camp and returns to their Westminster Farm. Seima and Seiko, the owners of the farm, begin to work for Gonzalo Mendez.

February 18, 1946—Judge Paul McCormick decides in favor of *Mendez, et al.* Garden Grove, Santa Ana, and El Modena School Districts file an appeal.

1946—Westminster School District integrates its elementary schools. The Mendez children enroll in Westminster Seventeenth Street School.

1946—The NAACP, American Civil Liberties Union, American Jewish Congress, and Japanese American Citizens League support the *Mendez* case on appeal by filing amicus briefs.

Dec 9, 1946—*Mendez, et al. v. Westminster* case is tried before the Ninth Circuit Court of Appeals.

January 1947—The Anderson bill is introduced to the California Legislature to end segregated education in California. It is passed by the State Assembly in April and by the State Senate in June.

April 14, 1947—The final decision by the Ninth Circuit Court of Appeals is handed down on *Mendez, et al. v. Westminster,* supporting Judge McCormick's ruling.

April 15, 1947—Jackie Robinson became the first Black major league baseball player, joining the Brooklyn Dodgers.

June 14, 1947—Governor Earl Warren signs the school desegregation bill into law.

September 1947—Schools in Garden Grove, El Modena, and Santa Ana are desegregated.

1950s—Johnson Intermediate School and Finley Elementary School, Westminster School District, are built on the Munemitsu Farm property, through the local government's use of eminent domain.

May 3, 1954—US Supreme Court holds that Mexican Americans are protected by the Fourteenth Amendment (*Hernandez v. Texas*).

1954—US Supreme Court rules that school segregation is unconstitutional in *Brown v. Board of Education.*

1964—Gonzalo Mendez dies at age fifty-one.

February 16, 1976—Executive Order 9066 rescinded by President Gerald Ford.

1978—Seima Munemitsu dies at age seventy-eight.

August 10, 1988—Civil Liberties Act signed by President Ronald Reagan.

1997—Masako Munemitsu dies in July at age ninety-three; Seiko "Tad" Munemitsu dies in April at age seventy-five.

1997—Dedication of Gonzalo and Felicitas Mendez Fundamental Intermediate School, Santa Ana, California.

1998—Felicitas Mendez dies at age eighty-two.

2003—Sandra Robbie produces *Mendez vs. Westminster: For All the Children/Para Todos los Niños.*

2007—US Postal Service issues *Mendez v. Westminster* commemorative postage stamp.

February 15, 2011—Sylvia Mendez receives the Presidential Medal of Freedom from President Barack Obama.

Family & Friends of This Story

The Mendez Family:

- Gonzalo and Felicitas Mendez, owners of the Arizona Cantina, Santa Ana, CA; community leaders against segregation in California public schools
- Sylvia Mendez, daughter of Gonzalo and Felicitas, Presidential Medal of Freedom honoree 2011
- Gonzalo Mendez Jr., son of Gonzalo and Felicitas
- Jerome "Jerry" Mendez, son of Gonzalo and Felicitas
- Sandra Mendez Duran, daughter of Gonzalo and Felicitas
- Phillip Mendez, son of Gonzalo and Felicitas
- Soledad "Aunt Sally" and Frank Vidaurri, sister and brother-in-law of Gonzalo Mendez
- Alice and Virginia Vidaurri, daughters of Frank and Soledad

Plaintiffs (parents' names only), *Mendez, et al. v. Westminster:*

- Gonzalo and Felicitas Mendez, Westminster
- Thomas and Mary Louise Estrada, Westminster
- William and Virginia Guzman, Santa Ana
- Frank and Irene Palomino, Garden Grove
- Lorenzo and Josefina Ramirez, El Modena

The Munemitsu Family:

- Seima and Masako Munemitsu, Japanese, first generation Issei, immigrants and farmers
- Seiko "Tad" Munemitsu, eldest son, married to Yone Sasaki Munemitsu
- Saylo Munemitsu, second son, married to Elizabeth Fairlie Munemitsu

- Akiko (Aki) Munemitsu Nakauchi, twin daughter of Seima and Masako, married to David Nakauchi
- Kazuko (Kazi) Munemitsu Doi, twin daughter of Seima and Masako, married to Satoshi Doi

Friends
- Mr. Frank Monroe, banker and friend of Tad and Gonzalo, First Western Bank, Garden Grove, CA
- Mr. David Marcus, attorney representing Mendez, et al. in *Mendez, et al. v. Westminster*

Key Advocates of the Story and Case
- Janice Munemitsu, daughter of Tad and Yone Munemitsu, author of *The Kindness of Color*
- Sylvia Mendez, daughter of Gonzalo and Felicitas, Presidential Medal of Freedom honoree 2011
- Sandra Robbie, alumni of Findley and Johnson Schools, Director/Producer of the 2003 award-winning documentary *Mendez vs. Westminster: For All the Children/Para Todos los Niños.*

BIBLIOGRAPHY

Books

Conkling, Winifred. *Sylvia & Aki*. Berkeley, Tricycle Press, 2011.

McLaughlin, David (author), and Ruben G. Mendoza (contributing editor). *The California Missions Source Book*. Pentacle Press, 2012.

Strum, Philippa. *Mendez v. Westminster: School Desegregation and Mexican-American Rights*. Lawrence, KS: University Press of Kansas, 2010.

Interviews

Mendez, Sylvia. Interview by Janice Munemitsu, July 29, 2019, Fullerton, California.

Nakauchi, Aki Munemitsu. Interviews by Janice Munemitsu, various dates.

Website Content

CRIT Films. *In Our Voice: The Chemehuevi, Hopi & Navajo Perspectives* (2018), fifty-five minutes, describes how four tribes came together on the CRIT reservation; and what a Japanese American internment camp had to do with it. https://www.critfilms.org.

Densho
https://www.densho.org

History
https://www.history.com

The History of Vaccines
https://www.historyofvaccines.org

Jackie Robinson
https://www.jackierobinson.com

Korematsu Institute
https://www.korematsuinstitute.org

Los Angeles Times
https://www.latimes.com

Merriam-Webster Online Dictionary
https://www.merriam-webster.com

National Baseball Hall of Fame
https://baseballhall.org

National Japanese American Memorial Foundation
https://www.njamemorial.org

The National WWII Museum, New Orleans
https://www.nationalww2museum.org

The New York Times
https://www.nytimes.com

Poston Preservation
https://www.postonpreservation.org

The Smithsonian Museum, National
Museum of American History
https://americanhistory.si.edu

VQR: A National Journal of Literature and Discussion
https://www.vqronline.org

Westminster School Dist. of Orange County, et al. v. Mendez, et al. No. 11310, Circuit Court of Appeals, Ninth Circuit, April 14, 1947, Document 161 F.2d 774 (1947). Visit http://cdn.ca9.uscourts.gov and search "Westminster School Dist. Mendez"

Other

Chapman University Library Archives

Hard copy of print article "Poston Pilgrimage: A Celebration in the Desert," from the *Tozai Times*, April 1985 (location: personal files of Janice Munemitsu)

Program from Poston Camp 1 Fifty-Year Reunion (1992) (location: personal files of Janice Munemitsu)

"Synopsis of Mendez v. Westminster, et al.," by Judge Frederick P. Aguirre (location: personal files of Janice Munemitsu)

ACKNOWLEDGEMENTS

I am so grateful for this God-sent community that partnered with me to bring *The Kindness of Color* to life.

The fond childhood memories of Sylvia, Gonzalo Jr., and Jerome Mendez initiated the reunion of our families. I am so thankful for your friendship over the years and to know Gonzalo and Felicitas through all of you. I spent so many wonderful visits with Sylvia and Sandra Mendez Duran, talking about these stories before I actually started to write them down. What a blessing it has been to document our shared history with your family.

I'm forever grateful for the legacy that my grandparents Seima and Masako, and parents Tad and Yone, and aunt Rakumi have given me through their "gambatte" spirit in overcoming adversity. Despite what they endured, they led our family forward with positivity and optimism. My aunt Aki Munemitsu Nakauchi partnered with me to document our story with her memories, and photos from our family archives. These times we shared of laughter and remembrance are a true treasure to me.

To Dr. Al Mijares and Dr. Jeff Hittenberger and the staff at the Orange County Department of Education, thank you for all the ways you encouraged me that this story is meaningful and will be significant for generations to come. The ongoing encouragement of Al and Jeff convinced me that our story was worthy to be shared as a book. Thank you for believing in me.

I knew little about publishing, so what a gift to work with the team that got this book from my laptop to a paperback! Special thanks to Drew Tilton of Asio Creative, who led me through the storyline development and the publishing process; your advice and guidance has been invaluable to me. I am so grateful to Jessica Snell, who thoughtfully and superbly edited the manuscript, polishing the text till it shined. Natalie Lauren Design created an inviting design that complements the story and offers hospitality to the reader. Thank you, Natalie! This team made sure this book welcomed the reader, page after page. I am especially grateful to reunite with May Angeles Brueckner for the cover; May took my vision for a symbolic illustration of kindness cultivating hope despite adversity and brought it to life. I am grateful for your sincere passion for this story that energized me throughout the process.

Special thanks to many dear friends for your encouragement and faith in this project, a project that chose me. The Oaks Center, Ramona, California, was a place of retreat which led me to refine my God-given calling, and gave me courage to do things far beyond what I could imagine. Thank you, Oaks Center team—I'll be back!

Finally, thank you to all who daily choose acts of kindness to each other, especially in the midst of adversity. Your commitment to kindness is cultivating hope for us all.

About Janice Munemitsu

Janice Munemitsu is a third-generation Japanese American Sansei. A native of Orange County, California, Janice worked on the family farm from age five through high school. She is a graduate of the University of Southern California and Biola University. Her family name, Munemitsu, 宗 光, means *source of light* in kanji. She hopes this book will be a source of light and hope, and will inspire us all to cultivate increasing kindness towards one another.

Childhood photo of author, Janice, with father, Tad, during strawberry season in the late 1950s.

About Sylvia Mendez

Sylvia Mendez is the daughter of Gonzalo and Felicitas Mendez, and a native of Orange County, California. As a young child in 1943, Sylvia was denied admission to the White public elementary school because of her Mexican heritage. She is a graduate of California State University, Los Angeles. In 2011, Sylvia was awarded a Presidential Medal of Freedom, the highest civilian award of the US, for her service as she encouraged students nationwide to value and complete their education—a service she continues to this day.

Author, Janice Munemitsu, and Sylvia Mendez wearing her Presidential Medal of Freedom, 2011.